MAKING GOOD DECISIONS: A BEGINNER'S GUIDE

MAKING GOOD DECISIONS

A BEGINNER'S GUIDE

BRIAN GROGAN SJ

VERITAS

Published 2015 by Veritas Publications
7–8 Lower Abbey Street, Dublin 1, Ireland
publications@veritas.ie
www.veritas.ie

ISBN 978 1 84730 631 9

10 9 8 7 6 5 4 3 2 1

A catalogue record for this book is available from the British Library.

Designed by Padraig McCormack, Veritas

Printed in Ireland by SPRINT-print Ltd, Dublin

Veritas books are printed on paper made from the wood pulp of managed forests. For every tree felled, at least one tree is planted, thereby renewing natural resources.

CONTENTS

ACKNOWLEDGEMENTS

Sincere thanks to my Jesuit mentors over the past sixty years, who helped me to catch on to the importance – and complexity – of discernment. A special mention must be made of John English SJ who apprenticed me in his workshops on the Ignatian Spiritual Exercises for the Corporate Person, and to Joe Veale SJ, whose wisdom is gathered in *Manifold Gifts* (Way Books, 2006).

Thanks also to the many who have inspired me by their efforts to live with discerning hearts, and to those who participated in workshops on decision-making which I have led over the years. My gratitude also to those who read through the manuscript in its various stages, encouraged me and made helpful comments: Phyllis Brady, Maria Duffy, Eileen Houlahan, Anne Lyons, Maura Lynch, Ann Martin, Pat Nolan and Orla O'Grady Walshe. Thanks also to Fiona Halpin for her secretarial assistance.

Thanks to Donna Doherty, commissioning editor, and to Daragh Reddin of Veritas, for their editing expertise.

PART ONE

PERSONAL DECISION-MAKING

CHOICES, CHOICES

✴ INTRODUCTION

The goal of this book is to help you to live to the full by making good decisions. Sometimes decisions come easily to us; at other times they are difficult to make. It is then that an unobtrusive wisdom-figure can be helpful, as the following story from Jane Fonda's engaging book *Prime Time* (Random House, 2011) illustrates.

Fonda had a friend, Jean Houston, whose parents had divorced when she was fourteen. The family was living in New York in the early 1950s. Jean was distraught by the family break-up, and to get out of the house and to get out of the house, took to walking her dog in nearby Central Park. There she met an elderly gentleman who gave his name as 'Mr Tayer'. Over the next eighteen months she encountered him a number of times. He was humorous, playful and imaginative, and their conversations made her realise she would eventually overcome the hurt experienced by her parents' divorce. She realised that for Mr Tayer, life was all about becoming, all about allowing yourself to be caught up in the rhythms of the universe. One day he said to her that while now she might be feeling like a caterpillar, she would soon become a butterfly. He asked, 'What sort of butterfly would you like to be?' She answered, 'I'll fly all over the world and maybe I'll help people. 'Ah, bon, bon, bon,' he replied. He told her that she could choose to live her life to the full rather than simply act out of a small portion of herself. She used to return home and tell her mother, 'When I'm with that man I leave my littleness behind.' After Easter 1955 he appeared no more. Years later Jean Houston happened to read *The Phenomenon of Man* and realised that the elderly gentleman had been none other than Teilhard de Chardin, a Jesuit priest and palaeontologist, one of the great minds of the twentieth century.

I like this story, especially because Teilhard de Chardin happens to be one of my favourite authors: I will often refer to him in the following pages.

Now you may not have the good fortune to meet such a mentor. But you can grow to share your life and your choices with none other than God, who knows your potential and wants to help you to live an exciting and worthwhile life. Each time you engage in a life-enhancing encounter with God your world opens out into a new and better space. That's the promise of this book.

NOTHING MAGICAL

In these pages we explore how we can come to make good decisions in our everyday lives. The word discernment means simply 'finding your way to good decisions'. My focus is on Christian discernment – coming to decisions prayerfully in the light of the Gospels. I will use the terms *decision-making* and *discernment* interchangeably. By communal discernment I mean the labour of a Christian group that is trying to reach its decisions prayerfully and together in the light of the Gospels.

There are hundreds of books already available on decision-making. They are written with leaders and managers in mind. This present book is different: it is written for those of us who may be neither leaders nor managers, but whose lives and choices are still of limitless importance, since each is a divine mystery and has a unique place in the unfolding of the world.

This work is different from a management book in another way. There is nothing magical about Christian decision-making: the process of discernment doesn't carry a cast-iron guarantee that you will be able to sort out all your problems neatly and efficiently. However, Christian discernment adds a new quality to the wisdom of the business world because it engages the divine dimension. God's wisdom and support help us focus on the choices under consideration. In this way, Christian decision-making is comprehensive: divine and human insights are harnessed. For example, when my mother suffered a severe stroke in 1985 there was no family member to look after her. She was a very private person who loved her home, but she could no longer manage alone. The notion of being consigned to a nursing home or hospice upset her deeply. She and I talked at length about the options without making progress until one day I came home and began talking about a workshop on discernment which I had just ended. She asked what discernment meant, and we got talking about God as being interested in all the decisions we make; that God helps us to choose what is best for us; that God stands by us then and enables us to cope with the consequences of difficult choices. Her eyes filled up: 'I never thought of God like that,' she said. She became peaceful and shortly afterwards agreed to go into a hospice. 'It will be my last address' she added bravely through her tears. She adjusted well to the hospice environment and lived out her remaining years in serenity. This was due not only to the good care she received, but to her new sense that God was close at hand: she felt safe. Consultancy is also hugely important in the business world: Christian discernment means the engagement of a divine consultant. In discernment I ask God directly, 'What do you think about this?' This approach presumes that there is a divine project for the world and every single one of its people. The divine agenda is indicated in the Gospels, most simply and unambiguously in the command: 'Love one another as I have loved you' (John 15:12). This command is not addressed to Christians alone: the command to act towards others as you would wish them to act towards yourself is known as the 'golden rule' and is embedded deep in human consciousness. The divine project is an all-inclusive community in which the dignity of everyone is respected. Discernment brings together divine wisdom and human goodwill, and this is the dynamic in which good decisions are most likely to emerge.

AUTHENTIC

I hope that this book will also be of interest to those who are not Christian. I am convinced from experience that wherever you stand on the scale of belief, you can reach good decisions by tuning into your deepest values – goodness, love, truth, compassion, kindness, the well-being of humankind – whatever brings you beyond the confines of the small self that looks only to its own concerns. No matter what flag of belief we wave – or none – we make good decisions only when we are *authentic* – by which I mean 'true to our best selves'. Authenticity or genuineness is one of the few traits that everyone can still acknowledge as valuable in today's pluralistic culture. When I use the term 'God' I signal my belief that there is a mysterious Other who is authentic and invites us also to be so. This Other is love, truth, compassion and kindness; it looks to the well-being of humankind and asks us to do likewise. Our deepest inner voice calls us to integrity and authenticity.

So with everyone of goodwill invited aboard, let us set sail to explore a very large sea. While we will touch on the managerial, social, psychological and other dimensions of decision-making, our main focus will be on the mysterious interplay between conscience and ourselves in the process. Even if you are an intuitive personality who says 'I go with my gut!' you may find it helpful to browse through the more analytic perspectives offered here.

WHY ANOTHER BOOK?

There is already a vast array of literature on discernment, which made me wonder why I should add to the list. I came to the conclusion that there was a gap in the humbler end of the market which I could help to fill – a treatment of decision-making that does not presume previous knowledge. The chapters that follow will, I hope, be helpful to anyone trying to make choices. I will cover a wider ground than is usually treated in books on decision-making, because my conviction is that every decision we make, whether macro or micro, has its own importance. To illustrate this, when writing this book, and taking into consideration its word-count limitations, I had to make a decision, however fleeting, about the suitability of every word I put down. This may seem over the top in regard to decision-making, but you do the same whenever you speak with or text someone. Each word plays its little part in shaping the world around us, as does each action or attitude. So the area for our study is vast.

While I can outline on paper what Christian decision-making looks like, it is my conviction that we fully understand it only in doing it. When faced with issues that affect our own lives, for example, when a partner considers a separation, a school faces a possible amalgamation, or a mother asks her daughter to move out – the hidden recesses of the heart can be laid bare and our motivations are seen in their true light. We learn a great deal about ourselves when we go through the discernment process, and we are all the better for it. We also learn a lot about others, and about God. You will know this in the making of your choices.

GETTING ADVICE

Open-minded people like to seek help when decision-making is difficult. This has been the way since humans first appeared and had to figure out how to make decisions. If I had lived two thousand five hundred years ago in ancient Greece I might have consulted the Delphic Oracle. In different cultures today I might seek an audience with the chief of the tribe, or the prophet, the shaman, the soothsayer, the medium. If I were a Quaker, a group of friends might gather round me, but not to offer advice: their task would be to ask me honest, open questions to help me discover my own inner truth around the issue that is bothering me. For Catholics, at least until Vatican II, all one had to do was to follow the teaching of the Church, a practice which was not so helpful because it largely ignored personal conscience and undercut individual responsibility. The slogan ran, 'Rome has spoken; the issue is ended.' This approach carries little weight among believers who have come of age since Vatican II and want to play their part as 'artisans of a new humanity' as the Council's Declaration on *The Church in the Modern World* puts it (n. 30). So where do you turn?

'KEEP GOD BEFORE YOUR EYES!'

This book is written from an Ignatian perspective. Throughout these pages, the name 'Ignatius' refers to Ignatius of Loyola, 1491–1556. He did not invent the art of Christian decision-making. His contribution to the topic is that of an articulator rather than an initiator. Ignatius had absorbed the long tradition of discernment that preceded him. He had a deep and intimate relationship with God, and was also gifted in analysing his own religious experience. He also had a facility for guiding searchers who were looking for help to lead good lives. Guiding people was one of his overriding concerns, a concern dating from his personal experience of floundering around in his own conflicting desires. He felt that he could do no better thing in life than to teach others how to find God and to notice God's promptings. He became a wisdom-figure, who, like de Chardin four hundred years later, provided enormous support for those who, wanted to live, not out of a small portion of their potentiality, but out of the fullness of their hearts.

His own early experiences in the area of decision-making were colourful and sometimes crude, but he learnt as he went. He was feisty, self-centred, abrasive, a womaniser, a gambler and on occasion hare-brained, as when, out of misguided loyalty to his king, he attempted the impossible in defending a broken-down fortress against the French. On another occasion, wondering whether he should kill a Muslim who doubted the perpetual virginity of Our Lady, he felt unable to make the right decision, and left it to his mule to decide. Today this would mean taking your hands off the steering wheel and letting events take their course! Happily the mule took a gentler path than the Muslim, so he and Ignatius both survived. If you want more on Ignatius, you can read my account in *Alone and on Foot* (Veritas, 2008).

ANY TIME, ANY PLACE

Over the years and with the active help of God, Ignatius fine-tuned the art of decision-making, and with a band of like-minded companions, founded the Jesuit Order in 1540. The Jesuits were an innovation in religious life – a group who would be available to serve God through active ministry. In the manner of the disciples sent out by Jesus, they would travel anywhere, engage in whatever enterprises God called them to, endure hardships and deprivation, all with the aim of serving people. Clearly, no external set of rules would suffice to keep such a group 'on track', given that they were to be explorers of the unknown. The rough and tumble of life, then as now, constantly uncovers bewildering new situations. Ignatius saw that the capacity for good decision-making would be crucially important, and while he set out guidelines and criteria for choices, his key advice was that Jesuits should always keep God before their eyes. That seems so simple, until you try it: then you become aware that it is easy to get fixated on your own performance or on the needs 'out there' so you forget all about what God might wish.

Ignatius was a man who had the gift of constructing concise phrases: these six words are loaded with spiritual dynamite. If the Jesuits kept their eyes on God, they would make good choices, so the order would fulfil what God might want of it. Their choices were to be God's choices; nothing less would do. God was to be for them what north is to the explorer using a compass. For Ignatius, God was not shadowy or remote but intensely present and active in the world. The early Jesuits filled their imaginations with the image of God who became human in Jesus. A recent study of Ignatius as leader argues that given his own great gift of imagination, he could identify other imaginative persons – people who could see in colour rather than in black and white, and who were at home in a multidimensional world. He invited them to soak in the images of the Jesus who walked the fields of Galilee, hung dying on a cross outside Jerusalem, and later, against all the odds, met his startled and forlorn disciples in the Last Supper Room, on the Emmaus Road, at the Lake of Galilee, and finally on the mountain, where they responded to his call, 'Go out into the whole world'. Once Ignatius felt that his companions had been won over by Jesus and had entrusted their hearts to him, he knew they could travel throughout the whole world and do whatever God would want of them.

It was not hard for the first Jesuits to decide that they should call themselves 'companions of Jesus'. The image of keeping Jesus before your eyes will serve you too on your own life's journey: you too are his companion. This makes God the steady point of reference in your decision-making.

DISCERNING ON THE GO

Important decisions often have to be made on the go. We don't always have the leisure of withdrawing from work and family life into a contemplative dimension in which we can deliberate with ourselves and God in tranquillity. Ignatian spirituality is realistic, and accommodates itself to our situations as busy people. We can be 'contemplatives in action'. Ours is often a noisy engagement with God, rather like someone trying to hear another person above the wind! God meets us where we are and adjusts to our pace. He helps us, as he helped the Emmaus-bound disciples, to 'catch on' to the deeper meaning of a situation. Persuaded by him, we make our decisions, as did those two disciples: they decided to abandon their evening meal and to go back to Jerusalem and so their lives were changed (Luke 24:13-35). In making decisions on the go, it helps to know that we have a divine companion who can keep up with us, who knows our story, listens well and can direct our hearts to the best choice.

Allow the various dimensions of good decision-making outlined in this book to touch you at the level of your heart and spirit, rather than merely at an intellectual level. Living a discerning life, walking your life's journey in divine company, is **a call to walk in mystery**. It means having the heart and mind of Jesus Christ – seeing as he did, having a heart like his, and responding creatively and courageously to emerging situations as he did.

God is to be the steady point of reference in our decision-making.

 # ELEMENTS IN DECISION-MAKING

DECISIONS

The word 'decision' comes from Latin and means 'to cut down'. When you make a decision to do something, you cut out other options. This can be frightening, and so we tend to postpone the fatal move, hoping that the situation will resolve itself. Sometimes it will if we procrastinate (which comes from the Latin 'to put off until tomorrow'), but that may lead to its own problems. When Pinocchio my cat had reached the end of his days, no one had the heart to put him down, even though he was in severe pain, and so he lingered on, enduring his diminishment stoically. Reflection and discussion of themselves will never 'produce' a decision. It is our deciding that brings reflection to an end. To decide not to decide is a decision! But how difficult it can be! Good decision-making is not always tidy. Consider the following example with which many parents will be familiar.

Sheila loves her grandchild Cathy, her daughter's only child. Her daughter and her partner split up soon after Cathy was born; neither of them was ready for the demands of parenthood, so Cathy has been living with her grandmother. Sheila has invested her life in Cathy, giving emotional and financial support, caring for her educational development, and acting as agony aunt when needed. But there are deep communication problems between them because of their conflicting views and values. Cathy's moods are expressed in anger, resentment, defiance, dismissiveness and abusive comments. Now twenty, she spends much of her free time with her current boyfriend and his family. She swings between despair of making anything of her life, and an arrogance that resists help. Her current prospects are limited. Although bright, she wasn't able to settle into study. She works in a supermarket – long hours for little return.

For months Sheila has wondered if it would be best for both of them if Cathy moved out. She feels that the endless hostility is doing neither of them any good, and that she is fostering an unhealthy dependency on Cathy. But she finds it hard to make the decision. She prays, 'God, help me! Show me what to do!' She wonders, 'What would Cathy do if I told her to go? Where could she live, with no proper income and no real friends or family?' Cathy was effectively abandoned by her parents as a small child: would she now feel her grandmother was abandoning her? Would this lead her into depression and a sense of hopelessness?

And so time passes, and they live together like hostile strangers much of the time. Is Sheila's a failed discernment? True, no neat solution is emerging, but discernment – like life – does not always work out. Freedom of personal choice can be very restricted where there is an emotional attachment to the other person involved, and that is how it is for Sheila.

It may be that without other viable options, Sheila is right to endure a bad situation for the present, while taking care of herself as best she can. This may seem like indecision, but in fact it is a decision, and it is made with the desire to do the best for Cathy and herself under the circumstances.

INNER FREEDOM

The interactions between Sheila and Cathy highlight the importance of inner freedom, so let's explore it.

Outer freedom is obvious enough – if I'm in jail or lying paralysed in bed I don't have it. Inner freedom is more subtle: for a start it helps to note the distinction between essential and *effective* freedom.

Stop for a moment and look back over the previous example in terms of freedom. Sheila and Cathy both have essential freedom – that's what being human means. But *effective* freedom depends on the particular situation. Unless Cathy has enough money and meets good people, her life will be very constricted. She won't be free to shape her life as she wants, and she won't grow to her full potential. Next, has Sheila the necessary inner freedom to let Cathy go, given the risks involved? Is she living out of messages she picked up when she herself was a child? 'Don't be selfish. Put other people's needs before your own. Parents sacrifice themselves for their children!' If she lives out of such messages Sheila's inner freedom becomes very limited and good decision-making becomes more difficult.

Cathy's moods clearly inhibit her inner freedom. Of all the elements in decision-making, the most important is inner freedom. Ignatius of Loyola saw this: he saw how people around him were making disastrous decisions because they were letting themselves be over-influenced by their emotions. They needed to get back on the firm ground of moral integrity. He was so caught by this that he devised his famous *Spiritual Exercises* to help people gain inner freedom so that their decisions would be made in a mature and unbiased way rather than from selfish motives. He thought it worthwhile that someone would spend thirty days in silence getting to grips with their wayward emotions, and that he, a busy man, would accompany them. His hope was that they would come to freedom of heart by getting to know what was going on inside when they were making their choices. He trusted that with this self-awareness, they could more easily allow God to lead them to their best decisions.

Ignatius suggests the image of a scales at equilibrium to indicate that we need to be well balanced if we want to make a good decision. Try using this image yourself when you are debating what to do. I notice that if one of my scales is piling up with anger or fear, I need to be wary of my choices until I calm down again. What look like choices can turn out simply to be poor reactions to situations. If I am in an exuberant mood, I can rush into decisions – such as splurging on a luxury item – without taking time to foresee the consequences. If I am a bit depressed, I can make decisions that are harsh to others and myself. One thinks of the boss who comes into the office after a row with his wife at breakfast, and blazes away at a bewildered worker. The earlier we can flag the fact that we are not 'at home with ourselves' the better our chances of regaining our inner equilibrium in a timely fashion.

Recent publications such as *The Discerning Heart, What's Your Decision?* and *The Way of Discernment* are all centred on Ignatian practices to help you develop inner freedom. Their details are given at the back of this book.

YOUR BEST CHOICE

How much time or income should my wife and I devote to the refugee issue?' 'I'm pregnant and I'm horrified. Should I marry my boyfriend?' 'Should I join the proposed strike for fair wages?' 'As an athlete, what about my taking performance-enhancing drugs as others do?' 'Should I drop out of the Church until it gets its act together about women's issues?'

Pause for a moment to notice some choices you need to make, and how you tend to make them.

On occasion we consider only our personal interests and ignore those of others, but mostly we try to make right decisions. We ask, 'What's the best thing to do in this situation?' We would be slow to deliberately make a wrong or immoral decision. Whether believers or not, we have a conviction about right and wrong; we hold to certain moral values. These values may differ from person to person, but still a sense of right and wrong prevails, or else society would have crumbled long ago.

Good people can, of course, make bad decisions without intending to. For example, over many centuries Christian churches tolerated slavery, and only slowly came to realise that slavery is a crime against human dignity. Today, in the Roman Catholic Church, the exclusion of women from its decision-making processes is unjust, but to break down that culture of exclusion is a mammoth task. The culture in which we live can encourage us to block out questions that need to be asked, and all but the prophetic few take the *status quo* for granted. We know this from family life: for many years as children we accepted unquestioningly the attitudes and values of our parents. But at some point we had to decide for ourselves what values we would live by. Mature decision-making involves reflecting on our assumptions in order to see if they are valid. Young people can think, 'Everyone smokes or drinks, so it's okay for me to do so.' Making a truly free decision can be difficult. It is demanding to ask: 'What is the wisest and most loving choice I can make in this situation?'

CONSCIENCE

Conscience literally means 'knowledge with'. It tries to catch the fact that I know what I'm doing as I do it. I am not acting simply out of instinct, nor do I haphazardly hit on what is right, like a monkey playing the piano. I have an inner sense of right and wrong, which I didn't construct for myself, but which is there to help me make right decisions. Until recently, conscience used to be restricted simply to our awareness of personal sinfulness. As children we were told, 'Go and examine your conscience, and then make your confession.' Conscience means our God-given ability to choose rightly. So it is our essential guide in decision-making. We are to follow it as best we can, at whatever cost. 'Its voice, ever calling us to love and to do what is good and to avoid evil, tells us inwardly at the right moment: do this, shun that' (Vatican Council II, *The Church in the Modern World*, n. 16). Without conscience, good decision-making would be impossible.

It is easier to live by slogans than to go through the demanding task of working out for yourself what is right and wrong. How do you react to the slogan, 'My country right or wrong!' or 'I was only obeying orders!' Surely to live like this would be to abdicate conscience and to betray your human dignity. Yet this is how terrorists and armies proceed.

On the other side you find the following: 'I'm a person of conscience. I do what I think best. I'm nobody's fool. Nobody can tell me what to do. I follow my own personal opinions!' To live like that is to be trapped within our private world. It fails to take account of the fact that we have much to learn from the wisdom of others. In exercising personal conscience we must maintain a diplomatic relationship with the consciences of those around us, while preserving our own integrity.

DEAD WORKS

I like the comment in the New Testament that the task of Jesus is to *purify our consciences from dead works to worship the living God!* (Hebrews 9:15). What might these 'dead works' be? I think of the dull repetitive actions that clog up our lives but have little life in them. I also think of an insight I once had – which I will relay later – which made me realise that what I had been doing in nurturing my perfectionism had been 'a great mistake'. Not only individuals but institutions such as churches can plod along dutifully piling up 'dead works'. The church in Sardis is told: 'I know your works: you have a name of being alive, but you are dead. Wake up!' (Revelation 3:1). Saint Paul talks of the 'good things' that we do which are useless because there is no enlivening love in them (1 Corinthians 13:1-3).

Our lives are intended to be love-inspired and directed towards the good of others; our gifts and talents are to be focused towards the service of the needy. Apparently most of us use only a small proportion of our human potential; we live out of *a tiny portion of our lives*, as de Chardin says. Jesus is someone who used up *everything* he had been given: that was how he brought such life to the world.

He is the example of what human beings can be when we abandon our 'dead works'.

CONSCIENCE FIRST!

Cardinal Newman – now on the path to canonisation – had a rich view of conscience. He was a prominent and respected member of the Anglican Church. But in 1845, at the age of forty-four, he became a Catholic. In doing so he was following his conscience, but he lost everything in the process – relatives, friends, position, honour and career. In making this demanding choice he had been forced to study the role of conscience deeply, and we can benefit from his labours. For example, he had to find a way to relay his high opinion of conscience to the reality of Church authority. He joked about this: 'If I am obliged to bring religion into after-dinner toasts (which indeed does not seem quite the thing), I shall drink ... to conscience first ... and to the pope afterwards.' He held that the Church and the pope are the servants of conscience, and that we must not abdicate conscience in the face of Church teaching. Conscience, he argued, is assisted and enlightened by revelation, by the scriptures and tradition, by the Church, and by the Christian community and others who bear witness to true values. But the Church must defend the freedom of everyone to follow their conscience, since God dwells in every heart and speaks to each individual.

Newman held that we could become convinced of the existence of God by becoming more fully aware of our conscience. He would ask, 'Where does the compelling power of conscience come from, unless from the One who created us?' God, he says, has an intimate personal relationship with each person, and speaks to them, directing them to good. His motto was 'heart speaks to heart' – the heart of God addresses our hearts. Conscience is a divine messenger from behind a veil: it is God whispering in the heart, if only we are willing to stop and listen. Through conscience we can recognise the living God active in our lives.

CAN I BE SURE?

Can I be sure that decisions made in good conscience please God? Suppose I do something that I sincerely believe to be right, but which turns out not to be? Does this spoil the plan of God? In response we can say that God's project is not pre-packaged: it is not an architect's blueprint which has a precise place for every brick and slate. It's an open plan, like the game plan of a football team manager. A good plan allows for maximum creativity within the objective of winning the match. God can integrate our errors and bring good out of them. Perhaps we can also say that God keeps moving the goalposts to our advantage. God wants us to exercise our precious gift of freedom: we are to be creative. A number of my friends who joined the Jesuits with me later left because they came to see that this way of life was not for them. We must believe that God is as interested in their alternative way of life as in their earlier one. For every decision we make God's major guideline is: 'Love one another!' So we must try always to make *loving* choices. And since God also gives us intelligence, each choice should also be as *wise* as we can make it. God doesn't ask more of us than that. I explained earlier that our question is to be: 'What's the wisest and most loving choice here?' That means, what will be for the best for the parties affected by this decision?

God doesn't get mad with us as we stumble along, doing what we believe is best yet making mistakes, especially in awkward situations. God respects us and accepts our decisions, whether they turn out good, bad or mixed, and God works within the new parameters which we create. 'Sure and certain' are perhaps not the most helpful terms to use about our decisions, which are always provisional to some extent. What matters is that we make our choices *with* God.

A well-intentioned decision is a leap of faith: it may turn out badly, but the important thing is that we are trying to listen to God and to shape our lives in relation to him. We become transformed in so doing. This was the path Jesus took: he didn't *know* that it was right to criticise the religious and political leaders of his time, but he believed he should, and so he did, though it led to his death. God chooses that we should walk in faith into an unknown future: this is messy and uncertain, but it keeps us close to God.

TRUST

In any good relationship we live by mutual trust and desire the other's good: it's the same in our relationship with God, when we explore the issue as best we can and then trust our consciences. In following a law we trust a human system: in following conscience we trust a divine Person. When God makes decisions, they are loving and wise: they are the best God can do in the concrete situations of our lives. Like God, we do the best we can. If we find out later that we could have made a better choice, then we reverse the decision if we're still free to do so. Every decision can be an act of drawing closer to God. If we can't alter a decision, we entrust the mess to God, as when a child says 'it broke!', they expect the parent to be able to mend whatever got broken.

God is always at work to bring good out of the disasters we create. From God's perspective, the possibilities for good are never exhausted, because nothing is impossible to God. God accepts our decisions. A decision closes off a world of possibilities, but even if we choose badly, God gives us new possibilities. Grace will accompany us to help us find God even when we are standing on the wrong path.

 At the end of the day each of us is left with ourselves, with our conscience and with the stirrings of the Spirit.

# CHRISTIAN DISCERNMENT

The word *discernment* has a long history. Again the term is a Latin one: *cerno* means 'to see', and *dis-cerno* means 'to judge the difference between things'. In the scriptures the term 'discernment' occurs thirty-three times. Sometimes it simply means wisdom, at other times it means the capacity to choose between right and wrong. But whether or not the term is used, you can read the whole Bible as a history of decision-making, a story littered with bad human decisions which God labours to correct, even at great cost. I will go into greater detail about this below.

People may imagine that the Jesuits spend their lives discerning what to do. But we do in fact get together regularly to see where we are going and where we think God wants us to go. Then we go off and try to live out that vision in our particular areas of work. For example, at a general congregation of the order in 1974, we came to see that when promoting faith we must also promote justice, because that's the way Jesus went about things. You might say it took us quite a long time to cotton on to this. But it's scary, and has led to the violent deaths of over fifty Jesuits in the past fifty years. Yet Christian decision-making must be faithful to the Gospel, whatever its demands.

THE MONEY CHANGERS

The early Christians used the image of money changers to explain the art of good decision-making. If the money changer was to stay in business, he had to develop a feel for the difference between a false coin that looked like gold and the genuine article. The underlying idea is from St Paul: 'Test everything and hold fast to what is good' (1

Thessalonians 5:21). Saint John warns his community not to believe every spirit, but to 'test the spirits to see whether they are from God' (1 John 4:1). To ensure that this tradition of discernment would survive, a phrase was attributed to Christ: 'Make yourselves into shrewd money changers.' With this authority behind it, the image of the money changers survived for a long time.

CHRISTIAN DISCERNMENT

Conscience can be distinguished from discernment, but they have much in common. If conscience helps us to distinguish right from wrong, discernment can be understood as bringing us to the level of distinguishing between good and better. Saint Paul advises his early converts 'to discern ... what is good and acceptable and perfect' (Romans 12:2). Choosing between two good options is the proper domain of Christian discernment. But sometimes it is not easy to notice the difference between what is good and what is, in fact, bad.

When we add the term *Christian* to the word *discernment* we move explicitly into trying to live as Jesus lived. Here we consult the Gospels and the Christian tradition to learn what best to do. Our concern is, '**What is the best thing to do in this situation in the light of the Gospel?**' We believe that God will guide us to a good decision if we ask and become receptive. The Holy Spirit works with us to help us make good choices. The Spirit gives light and strength, and brings us to the truth if we are willing to be led. The Spirit is behind all true discerning, whether the person invokes God or not.

CASTING YOUR VOTE

To live in a democracy means we decide many social and political issues by public vote, as in a general election, or a referendum regarding entry into the EU, or legislation on same-sex marriages, abortion and euthanasia and so forth. Here issues of morality may become central. How do we make a good decision? The proposed legislation may be highly complex, the facts may be hard to grapple with, and the counter-arguments proposed by reputable persons may be confusing. You do your best to inform yourself on the issue; you ponder the issue in the light of the Gospel; you may consult the rich social teaching of the Church. You try to hold yourself at equilibrium and ask God to lead you to the best option.

But it isn't easy. Our family always voted Fine Gael, so I can remember the consternation when my elder brother announced at the age of sixteen that he'd be voting Fianna Fáil. A world collapsed for me – now I'd have to make up my own mind about who to vote for! I needed inner freedom to consider standing against the family tradition, but I also needed to know the facts.

Likewise as the world and the Church changed I had to blow the dust off many assumptions to see if they were still valid. I was ordained in 1968, in the month when the encyclical *Humanae Vitae* appeared, condemning artificial birth control and contraception. The day before I headed off to give my first homily, I rang the parish priest to learn his view of the encyclical. 'You're on your own, Father!' was his response! And I was; I wasn't invited back ...

In my youth the Church said nothing about caring for the environment, but now I need to look at *Laudato Si'* and let it colour my thinking. For instance, it explains how every purchase is a moral decision, not simply an economic one. Strolling in shopping centres will never be quite the same again! The next time you head out for some 'retail therapy' think of going shopping with God ...

DISCERNING CAN BE LIFE-CHANGING

All choices are important. But choices made by persons in power can alter the lives of many people and change the course of history. Harry Truman as President of the US decided in August 1945 to launch the atom bomb on the people of Japan in order to end the war in the Pacific. His options in the months leading up to the fateful decision were difficult: should he allow the war to continue rather than use a weapon of mass destruction? Or would lives ultimately be saved by forcing the Japanese to surrender after the destruction of one of their cities? If the bomb were dropped in an unoccupied area to demonstrate its destructive power would the Japanese simply fight on?

Our purpose here is not to pass judgement on Truman but to highlight the need for decision-makers to consult the One who cares for all sides in a conflict.

SHAPING GOD'S WORLD

In a serious choice, many dimensions of life can come into question. It is God's people and God's world I am dealing with in making it. But what do I know even about myself, not to mention God and God's people? Add in the level of my personal freedom: am I fairly predetermined or like a balance at equilibrium, or somewhere in between? Am I sensitive to the deeper human issues? Have I any feeling for the language of the heart in which God speaks to me? On the spectrum of awareness of God's engagement in my life, would I be nearer to zero than to a hundred? In short, am I up to speed in making my choice?

How do I know what is best for those who will be affected by what I decide? Recently I had to help clear out a house belonging to a friend who had developed dementia. What to keep and what to throw out? A decision had to be made about each thing, one by one. Our little group was exhausted at the end of it all, nor had we the comfort of knowing that we had done the 'right thing' about each item. As the skip got piled higher and higher, I found myself asking pardon of my friend for dismantling his life. The line from Julian of Norwich kept coming into my head, 'All will be well, and all manner of things will be well' and I prayed to believe it, but I didn't feel it. I made up my mind to jettison my own unwanted cargo before the time came when decisions would be beyond me.

I first explore the dynamics involved in making *personal* decisions;

in the second part of this work I go on to apply these dynamics to *group* situations and meetings, because it is there that many important decisions are made. How can we play a constructive role in them? I propose that, when as Christians we attend a meeting, we are to be spokespersons for God. **God's concerns are to be ours.** God wants our help to ensure that the decisions which emerge from meetings are truly wise and good. Essentially, good decisions help to build inclusive community. As I write, thousands of refugees are trying to cross the Mediterranean to get to safety in Europe: each of them is important to God, who commands us to 'welcome the stranger'. The question becomes: 'What ought we do about this human tragedy?' If I were a refugee, what could I hope for from you? When you answer that question, you may well find your conscience saying to you, 'Go and do likewise!' (Luke 10:37).

THE HUMAN WEB

No decision is purely private. What I decide shapes me in some way, and so it shapes the world, since I am part of the world. Each of us is 'a child of the universe' and whether we intend it or not, our choices make a difference, at least to some degree, to those around us. We live in a web of relationships, and we can't wriggle out of that web and stand alone. We do not live in self-enclosed bubbles. As the poet John Donne wrote, 'No man is an island'.

All our decisions have a ripple effect. In making them we either contribute to or diminish the well-being of those around us. This is because God, the author of reality, is not a solitary figure on a throne but a God of relationships, so we are destined for relationships. We are closer to others than we think, and God works to integrate our personal choices with what is best for the wider world. With one hand God guides us uniquely and individually; with the other, God shapes our common destiny to bring us all into eternal joy. It is within the community of humankind that we become what we are meant to be.

Good decisions build relationships and community. Poor decisions divide people. For the human story to unfold as God intends, we need to play our part by making good choices. God supports our efforts to do this; God engages with us in this task. Discernment is about this divine-human collaboration. God loves me, my neighbours and my world, and since my decisions affect myself and those close to me, I am called to make my choices in a spirit of love. Otherwise, I spoil the delicate dynamics of God's work in the world. Some time ago an energetic and talented woman told me the following:

> I was in the habit of using the phrase, 'This is no concern of mine' to excuse myself from getting my hands dirty. I'm a Christian, but I wanted life to be a safe affair, and I had my security blanket tightly wrapped around me. Then one day at a retreat the speaker talked about the notion of finding God in everything. I'd heard that phrase often before, but this time my 'private' life burst open and I saw the real world for the first time – it was a bit like coming out of a tomb into the sunshine. My slogan got turned inside out: if I'm to be a Christian 'this *is* a concern of mine' – the needs of people ARE my concern. It's scary and risky to get involved, but now I'm open for business and life is full of colour.

 We fully understand discernment only by doing it.

A WORLD OF POSSIBILITIES

You may be familiar with the 'butterfly effect', which posits how a small event somewhere in the universe may touch off a major event in another. The 'butterfly effect' is an image coined by Edward Lorenz in 1972. He asked, 'Does the flap of a butterfly's wings in Brazil set off a tornado in Texas?' and considers how events, small and insignificant in themselves, can alter history and shape destinies. So the question arises, 'How far do my seemingly private decisions alter the shape of reality around me?'

We would, I think, agree that our macro decisions have far-reaching effects. President Truman's decision to use the atom bomb in 1945 ended the war with Japan, for instance, but brought us into a new era of destructiveness. The decision of God to enter the world in person changed the shape of human history and of all creation. But what about those micro decisions we make, the ones we hardly notice?

'AND SO I DECIDED ...'

Watch young children – from early on they make small decisions, which build into patterns of behaviour. The child *decides* to scream when there is no parent in sight, or to be unkind to a sibling. Our personalities are built up little by little by our choice of one possibility over others at any given moment. We live in a world full of possibilities. So when I *decide* to get up in the morning, one possibility out of several is actuated. I could have decided to stay in bed, or get up later, or called into the office to say I was sick. So every action or reaction in my day results from a *decision*. For each step I take, each word I say, each item I attend to, there were other possibilities I could have considered.

As I mentioned earlier, Pope Francis, in his encyclical on the environment, makes the following startling statement: every purchase we make is a *moral decision* rather than simply an economic one (*Laudato Si'*, n. 206). But if it is a moral decision I need to evaluate it rather than make it spontaneously. How many small decisions I make in a day I don't know, but each of them helps to colour and shape me and the world around me, as *Laudato Si'* ably illustrates.

The 'Serenity Prayer' was written by Reinhold Niebuhr, Lutheran pastor and theologian (1892–1971). Used by innumerable people across the world, it is a prayer to make good decisions.

> *God, grant me the serenity to accept the things I cannot change,*
> *Courage to change the things I can,*
> *and the wisdom to know the difference.*
> *Living one day at a time; enjoying one moment at a time;*
> *accepting hardship as the pathway to peace;*
> *taking, as He did, this sinful world as it is, not as I would have*
> *it. Trusting that He will make all things right if I surrender to his*
> *will;*
> *that I may be reasonably happy in this life, and supremely happy*
> *with him forever in the next. Amen.*

This most practical of prayers shows that making good decisions can be a moment-by-moment affair, not a practice to be resorted to only on rare occasions. One drink can have disastrous and wide-reaching effects. Jesus illustrates God's concern for detail in a graphic way by saying that every hair on our heads is numbered and that not one sparrow falls without God's being aware of it (see Luke 12:6-7). Likewise each decision, even if small, has a divine significance, so we do well to check our choices with God.

NOTHING NEW?

Looking at the same issue from another angle, we can think of reality as being 'out there'- independent and solid, like a dog or a house. But is reality already fixed and impervious to change? If so, we can make little impact on the world around us, and so we can think of ourselves as 'victims of circumstance'. Life becomes hemmed in, limited to a small range of choices. Things appear dull and predictable. Each day becomes the same as the last. The sacred writer of long ago seems to have felt this: 'What has been will be again, what has been done will be done again; there is nothing new under the sun' (Ecclesiastes 1:9). He had no sense of the world being charged with possibility!

The story goes that about AD 1500, when Columbus came in sight of the West Indies, the Indians on the shore could not at first see his ships because they had no previous awareness of such things. For them, Columbus' fleet simply wasn't there! Things can be before our eyes but the brain cannot accommodate them. We build up models of reality and settle for the predictable. If you were convinced that the moon is made of cheese, you would waste your costly moon voyage desperately taking samples to prove you are right, and you would miss the thrill of exploring what the moon actually is.

WHAT DO YOU SEE?

Must life be routine, narrow and dull? Not at all! If my life is grey, it is because I decide to paint it that colour. It is my experience that those - especially in the Church - who decide to live by rule, rubric and regulation are less than happy. They have cut out much of the mystery of life so that they can manage and control it, so life holds no happy surprises for them. What image they have of God I do not know, but there is a better one - the image of the One who makes all things new (Revelation 21:5). I slid out of bed this morning into a world of divine possibility, if only I can see it as such. Boredom is not a fact of life but the fruit of inner decay. It is a misguided understanding of reality. I can understand my world in a different way. When I do, a fresh world of options opens out for me like a fan. Even if I am bedridden and limited to a confined environment I can decide to change my attitude to my environment – to the world outside the window, to the nurses, fellow patients and visitors who come by, to the food and drink provided for me; I can choose to listen to the news on the radio and to pray for those who are suffering. Life is always pulsing with energy, and I can tap into it.

WHAT'S THE MEANING?

We assign meanings to our experiences from the time we are infants. This helps us to cope with the world around us, but it can also condemn us to making the same response to all situations that appear identical but in fact are not so. One bad experience with an authority figure – parent, neighbour, teacher - can lead us to fear all authority figures. Thus, we lose our freedom to face each moment and situation with clear minds. We may need help to discover the root cause of our unfreedom. Why do I tend to have a set view on certain things and people? Do I draw only on past understandings, or do I look to future possibilities?

SHAPING THE FUTURE

As the Benedictine monk Mark Patrick Hederman states in *The Haunted Inkwell*, (Columba Press, 2001), we shape the future by our choices; there is no pre-set future out there. Reality is not static, it is bursting with possibilities. The future will repeat the past only if we are not open to change. But if we create our future we must learn the art of making good decisions. Hederman would say that to do this we need to get in touch with artists, poets and holy people because they are more in touch with the Ultimate than the rest of us. They offer something more, something of the Truth. They are close, as Gerard Manley Hopkins' says in 'God's Grandeur', to 'the dearest freshness, deep-down things'. We can also get free of our preconceptions by reading the Gospels with fresh minds. God's point of view is always new.

Quantum physics invites us to look at everything in terms of possibilities rather than as static facts. All reality is ultimately the product of the thought or consciousness of God. But God's thinking is always fresh: God is busy about creation today. And human consciousness has its own creative power. As John Milton wrote in *Paradise Lost*: 'The mind is its own place, and in itself can make a heaven of hell, a hell of heaven.' You help to shape the reality of your world by your thinking and your decisions. You decide to take a certain attitude or mood towards things, and this creates a new situation. As people think, so they are (Proverbs 23:7).

Just as you customise your computer, in an analogous way you can customise your day and your very self, through your thinking and deciding, because thoughts are *real*, and decisions are *real*! If you think gloomy thoughts they become part of your reality.

A NEVER-BEFORE DAY

You can instead decide to see each day as a 'never-before' day, and live it as such. 'Every day a good day' is a Zen saying. The sun never played on the water in this glass in quite this way before; that smile from a friend is freshly minted; never before were the clouds shaped and coloured quite the way they are today; and it never rained quite like this before! As the philosopher Heraclitus said two thousand five hundred years ago, you cannot step into the same river twice. Everything is in process of change, and we can have a hand in the process. The details of my life are the raw material for good decision-making.

Each day you can say to yourself, 'I'm having one of these never-before days!' – and mean that *positively*. If someone asks you, 'anything strange?' you can ask them how long they have to listen, because *everything* is strange. Things can go dreadfully wrong and the world is full of victims of malice. But this can either beget in me a passive endurance or become a challenge to shape things better. I am not condemned to replay my bad tapes over and over. I can get off my treadmill and walk a new path. I can take control of my life through my attitudes. I can ask, 'what will I do today?' I may indeed do my ordinary work, but now with a new charge and energy, because instead of things 'just happening' I am *deciding* to do what I do, whether to drive a bus, teach a class or look after a disabled family member. I can interpret people positively to others, rather than running them down. I can be gentle with my inadequate self when I have messed things up. I can *decide* to stand poised in God's evolving world, or to become one of the 'left behinds' of evolution. The art of mindfulness has much to teach us: it focuses the body and mind on the present, so that we can concentrate on what is happening right now and draw energy from it.

A SURPRISING GOD

When God enters our world in the person of Jesus, astonishment and surprise are the order of the day. Jesus amazes the crowds by his fresh way of thinking and seeing, and by the extraordinary things he does for people. He seems to take it for granted that he is living in a world of possibilities, and that he can decide which are best to choose. He was, I believe, trying to liberate our thinking and our presuppositions about ourselves, about others and about God. To those who believed in him he gave power so that they might become nothing less than the *sons and daughters of God* (John 1:12). Think of the change of attitude to yourself this can bring. Theologians speak of the shock the Hebrews experienced by bumping into God, and every scene in the Gospels portrays the shock of encounters with the divine. God is always 'doing a new thing', and wants us to catch on (Isaiah 48:6). So I can live in a world of surprise and grateful amazement: it's my choice!

ALL THINGS NEW

Prayer becomes alive when we are open to God's surprises. Day after day we can say to God, 'Surprise me!', and it happens. Adrienne von Speyr, a twentieth-century mystic, imagined that before the Fall everything was fresh and unexpected to Adam and Eve. After the Fall, with the darkening of their minds, experience became predictable and dull. In her view our task is to get back to original freshness, to let God surprise us at every turn. Was Jesus saying to us, 'unless you become as little children you are missing the point?' For babies everything is new and deserves exploration. But we lose this primal curiosity and become creatures of habit. We then stagnate and become no more than half-alive. Our compulsions and addictions, assumptions and presuppositions, can dominate our choices.

Hard work is needed to become free of our small mental constructs. We begin to gain freedom when we cotton on to the world of possibilities that surrounds us. Long ago Moses faced the chosen people with a decision: 'choose life or death!' But the same challenge is ours, day by day. With God we can become co-creators of our future. Fresh decisions can shape our lives into a new openness; discernment is a matter of choosing between an optimal and a minimal level of life. 'With God, everything is possible' – this awesome statement forms a motif that runs through the scriptures from Genesis on. In our own way share we in this world of possibility that God inhabits. Let's grow our imaginations!

 The future is alive with possibility to the extent that we are open to change.

CASE STUDY: A GREAT MISTAKE

The following story is drawn from my own experience.

Like many others I joined religious life in the 1950s because I wanted to do 'the better thing'. I inhabited the world of the perfectionist. I wanted to be better myself, and to make the world better. I said to myself, God is perfect after all, and aren't we meant to be like 'our heavenly Father'?

Driven by a somewhat warped mode of Jesuit formation, I started trying to improve my companions who I felt were not measuring up to what we were meant to become. Without intending it, I made them feel bad about themselves. I was not loving them – nor myself – in our common limitedness and inadequacy. And I believed God could love me only insofar as I was at least 'striving for perfection'.

My wake-up moment came in the form of a dream. In the middle of a psychotherapy session I recounted a dream about my mother lying on a bier: she looked perfect, but she was dead. He stopped me at that point: 'Dead? Perfect?' He closed the session there and then (though he charged me for the full session, which irritated me!). Driving home, I suddenly saw the point and burst out laughing. 'It's all been a great mistake!' I said to myself. 'I've put in fifty years trying to be perfect, and I've been killing myself and others in the process. Perfectionism and death go hand-in-hand! But I don't have to live like this!' A world of well-intentioned but misguided striving began to dissolve. This was one of the great moments of liberation in my life. However, I'm still working towards fuller liberation, because this perfectionist compulsion had its origins in a somewhat dysfunctional family set-up which I internalised in my early years, so its roots are deep. But now

I believe I am loved as I am, in my enduring inadequacy, and that the challenge is not to become 'perfect' but simply to love others in their inadequacy too.

MY COMMENTS

> Dreams are important: they allow difficult things to surface which our conscious mind represses, because there may be too much at stake – perhaps a total reversal of values, a change of life. We may need other eyes than our own to see the point because we suffer from blind spots. These can build up when we ignore unwanted insights around areas of behaviour or attitude. The truth is always trying to get through to us, but we keep slipping away from it.

> Why does God let us drift so long in compulsive patterns that damage ourselves and others? God could presumably sort us out in an instant, but in fact shows great respect for our slow pace of development. God's patience with my tardy growth has helped me to respect the unique pace of growth of those around me. The parable of the wheat and the weeds means a lot to me now: 'let them grow together until the harvest!' (Matthew 13:20).

> I floundered for a while as I began to get untangled from my perfectionist style. If perfectionism was not the way, then what is? What about St Teresa of Ávila's book, *The Way of Perfection*? I was helped by another book, this one by Ernest Kurtz and Katherine Ketcham called *The Spirituality of Imperfection*. Its point is that our very nature is to be *imperfect* – only the creator is perfect. I learned elsewhere that the injunction 'be perfect!' (Matthew 5:48) could be more happily translated to mean: 'Be compassionate, become whole, be yourself!'

> Some years ago I wrote a book called *To Grow in Love: A Spirituality of Ageing* (Messenger Publications, 2011). The title was borrowed from a phrase in the liturgy, 'Make us grow in love'. I now see my life project, or should I say, God's project for me, in terms of

growing in love. There is nothing very startling about that, but what matters is that I have come to see it as centrally important.

➤ How many small decisions had combined over the years to form this deep pattern of perfectionism in me, I do not know. I am more aware of the struggle to move in the opposite direction – the patient acceptance of 'flawedness' in myself and others. Only slowly do small decisions to resist former mental stances merge into patterns and habits, then progress towards the light becomes easier and more spontaneous.

➤ My moment of insight was not violent but gentle – a good sign that it was coming from God. For the most part, God labours delicately over us, encouraging us to engage our shadow sides, coaxing us to let go of the weapons and defences that stood us in good stead in our earlier years. God wants us to become our true selves.

YOUR COMMENTS

_____

_____

_____

_____

_____

_____

 'I'm free! I don't have to live like this!'

 # DESIRES

Choices emerge out of desires, so let's look at our desires. When I was young, desires used to be understood as referring mainly to the sexual dimension of our lives. 'Impure desires' were a primary issue in preparing for confession. Now the word has been liberated to refer to all our wants, wishes, needs, preferences, the things we have our hearts set on. 'If I had this or that, I'd be happy!' Things pull at us in various directions, and so desires play a big role in decision-making.

We are a jumble of desires. I like peace and quiet, but also the company of friends. I like to be accepted. I desire health, and a reasonably long life – I catch myself asking: 'just a few years more, Lord, please!' I want to live in modest comfort, and I also want to help the needy who have so much less than myself. I want to be happy, and want others to be happy. I want to play even a small part in building a better world. I want to be close to God, and to be pleasing to him. I want eternal life, and I want everyone else to be included in it.

Take a moment to think about your own 'bucket list' of desires. This will help you to recognise that when you come to make a decision, there may be a lot of personal factors that influence the process. You may not be as free as you would wish. Desires are an unruly mob, and they need to be orchestrated and prioritised or else life will be chaotic.

'WHAT DO YOU WANT?'

Good desires are implanted in us by God. To take a striking example: when Jesus meets with his first would-be disciples, he doesn't start preaching at them. Instead he puts them in touch with their desires by asking them: 'what do you want?' (John 1:38). In other words, 'what is your desire? Do you know what you are looking for?'

The precondition for a good decision is that I want to make a wise and loving choice. This seems so obvious, but I may in fact be quite determined that whatever choice is made, it must at least *please me*, whatever about pleasing God or others. So, are my desires well-ordered, in harmony with right living and the guidelines given by Jesus in the Gospels? Or are they disordered, such that I am looking out first for myself? How much inner freedom have I around my conflicting desires when a tough decision is looming? It is good to have desires, otherwise we are less than fully alive, but they can dominate our freedom – we are easily knocked off-centre. But by taking time out to reflect, we can become aware that we are being 'got at'. So we can adjust and return to that poised freedom or equilibrium that we spoke of earlier.

THE DESIRE FOR GOD

Everyone desires happiness, and the art of becoming happy lies in making the best choice between the welter of options that demand attention. Believers try to hold to the conviction that their happiness lies in God, the author of all happiness. In making decisions they try to put into second place the desires that conflict with this basic longing for God. Ignatius of Loyola wanted to help people to become free of their unhelpful attachments, so as to be able to choose wisely. He loved to work with people of great desires, because when their desires are well-orchestrated they would do great things. In the Gospel, Jesus meets a rich young man and is very taken by his goodness of heart: he invites him to give all his wealth away and follow him. But the young man's desire to keep his wealth wins out. He goes away 'sad' because he knows he has betrayed his best self. We know the feeling: to be a disciple of Jesus is a fine thing – but then it makes difficult demands, and we find ourselves torn. Think of the choice Christians had to make in face of Nazism in World War II. Most turned a blind eye to what was going on. We can criticise them, but what would you or I have done?

LOVE CHANGES EVERYTHING

When I am in love, I get joy in choosing the things that please the other person, even if this involves a sacrifice for me. I want to be in solidarity with the other. But this can bring me into totally uncharted territory: if I were to love the victims of injustice, how radically might that stir up my life? At least my heart might go out to them, and I would pray for them, and who knows what that might achieve? As Tennyson writes: 'More things are wrought by prayer than this world dreams of.' Such prayer for others is a form of caring, and it brings me closer to God and to those I am asked by Jesus to love. As another writer puts it: 'this pool of private charity must flow a world-embracing sea.' My development means that slowly I become a person of great love. Nothing less than this is the goal that God has for me as a cherished member of the family of God. When God comes to preside in my heart, then love colours all my efforts to make good decisions. Prayerful pondering of scripture is an opening of the door that opens out into the imagination of God. I then wrestle with God until my own constricted imagination embraces to some degree that alternative world that God has in mind, a world in which love embraces all.

 The precondition for a good decision is that I want to make a wise and loving choice.

CASE STUDY: TAKING A RISK

I have looked at the stances taken in regard to the world around us, and have noted the importance of those tiny decisions that conspire to build up in us an integrated or a distorted world view. We can now ask, 'what does good decision-making look like in the concrete?' Our micro choices can often be too subtle to analyse, so we get a better perspective by reviewing choices that are spread over time and involve serious reflection. The following decision takes in elements that I have looked at thus far: conflicting desires, inner freedom, openness to new possibilities, conscience, the wisest and most loving thing to do, and so forth.

In 1981 I was asked to go to Somalia for a short period. Now Somalia is not the first place you'd think of for the holidays, so first I had to locate it on the map – East African coast, with its capital, Mogadishu, on the Equator. Somalia is a Muslim country, and all but four missionaries had been expelled when the communists took over, seven years earlier. Congregations of Sisters were allowed to remain only because the Somali authorities thought highly of them as nurses and teachers. But they were unwilling to stay unless there were priests to provide them with the sacraments. So the Archbishop of Mogadishu got in touch with the Jesuit Superior General, Pedro Arrupe, who had founded the Jesuit Refugee Service (JRS) a year earlier. The archbishop wanted a priest to test whether the authorities had eased their restriction on priests entering the country. Would some Jesuit be willing to be a guinea pig?

I was in transition between two administrative posts at the time. I was supposed to be taking things easy, and it was impressed on me that I should feel free to turn down the Somali proposal. After all, no one knew what might happen.

There were four possible outcomes if I went: I might be denied entry on arrival; I might be jailed, with or without charge; I might become one of the 'disappeared'; or I might be allowed to stay and so accomplish my mission. And if I did not go, needy Somalis would not receive from the Sisters the help they badly needed.

How healthy was my inner freedom? Since Jesuits are meant to be available for service anywhere in the world, and since I don't like to let people down, I found in my heart a basic willingness to go. But my emotions were elsewhere! Fear dominated my horizon, largely by night but often by day. Could I do this? How would I survive, without a word of Somali, without knowledge of the Muslim faith, without experience of fending for myself? Suppose I fell sick? The four priests in the country spoke only Italian, so how would I communicate with them? My demons ran riot.

I consulted a few people who knew me better in some ways than I know myself. They were careful to respect my freedom of choice but provided a forum for me to talk things out. I talked with God too and asked for the courage to be free to go. I weighed the arguments for and against, as best I could. I asked God to move my heart in the right direction, and slowly I found more peace in saying 'I'll go!' than in turning down the request. So I went.

When I got to Rome I met Pedro Arrupe, the leader of the Jesuits, who had suffered a major stroke two months earlier and had lost the power of speech. When I told him I was off to Somalia he raised a hand and shouted out one word: 'Go!' I scuttled off, confirmed in my mission. If this was not a sign, what was? But that afternoon news came that my sister-in-law in Dublin had taken her own life, and the family naturally wanted me be with them and to look after the funeral. Was that a contrary sign? I flew back to Dublin, totally confused.

But I found that my decision to go still felt right, and four days later I set off again, eventually arrived in Mogadishu, and was allowed a three-month stay. It was lonely there; everything was strange; the heat was intense. But Arrupe's command, 'Go!' kept ringing in my ears, and letters from friends at home eased the isolation.

What good my brief presence did for the people I had come to serve I do not know. As C.S. Lewis remarks, 'God tells no one any story but their own'. Political and military turmoil devastated Somalia shortly after I left; my host, the Archbishop, was murdered and the cathedral was burnt down. The tiny Christian population of some three hundred was scattered. But my own story was changed radically: I came to a new compassion for the plight of those who live at the bottom of the human pyramid, and that was good.

MY COMMENTS

➢ When the issue first arose, I wonder how free I was to say, 'no'. Was I driven rather by my inclination to please people? Praying for openness and also for inner freedom saved me from making a decision until my fears had been allayed.

➢ I had the overall desire to do what God might want, even at a cost, which was good. But I remember looking for certainty in choosing to go. I wished that God would appear before me and say 'Go!' God, however, waited until I had decided, then left it to Pedro Arrupe to dispel my lingering doubts.

➢ The sense of stepping into the unknown was strong, given the meagre information that I had gathered about Somalia, and I experienced the tugs of contrary emotions, what Ignatius calls 'consolation' and 'desolation'. I thought in turn about the security of the institutional life I had had heretofore in the Jesuits, and then of the excitement of breaking out into something new.

- The peace that finally came prevailed over considerable surface disturbance, and I can only ascribe it to God. I came to trust that God would be with me in the project, however it might unfold.
- My trip brought no tangible success to the poor population of Somalia. But on another level something good emerged – the conversion of my heart to the poor of the world. I think Plato is right: life is a risk, but a beautiful risk!

YOUR COMMENTS

_____

_____

_____

_____

_____

_____

_____

 Decision-making is demanding, but a Mysterious Other is present to support our efforts.

THE
LANGUAGE
OF THE HEART

NOTICING INNER STRUGGLES

We have seen that when we look inside ourselves a little, we often notice conflicting mental states. Our private world of emotions, feelings, and thoughts is a busy one, as psychologists and therapists know. We may find that we are caught in 'mood wars', torn this way and that, perhaps in ways that are not a little shocking, as when we find ourselves raging with someone whom we also deeply love. In ordinary conversation we speak of our *hang-ups*. Psychologists discuss *compulsive and inhibitory patterns of behaviour*. Spiritual writers in the past used to list our *inordinate attachments* and *capital sins*. Whatever terms we use to name the obscure forces within, we need to be able to recognise them.

> Barbara is speaking: 'I have come to notice with surprise that I'm developing negative feelings towards my partner. He's becoming insensitive towards me. I wonder if perhaps he doesn't really love me anymore? But when I start on this track, it leads me to feel insecure, which in turn leads to cold anger, with occasional outbursts that spoil our home life. I can spend hours in free fall, negative images crowding one another like bluebottles feeding off a lump of dead meat. I hate myself for this, but once the negative is triggered I can't stop.'

Feelings and emotions in themselves are neither good nor bad – they are simply there, like clouds in the sky. But among the psychological phenomena that play on the heart, we can identify some that lead us in a good direction, and others that lead us in the wrong direction. Jokingly we may say, 'The devil made me do it!' This points to a deep truth: when we act against our reason, we are being gripped by something that is not our best self. So we blame someone else, as Eve does: 'The serpent tricked me and I ate' (Genesis 3:13). We can say, 'I don't know what led me to do that'. But what is this 'what' which can lead us astray? Let's be slow to blame the snake! Sin in scripture is understood as our tendency to 'miss the point' – and the point we miss is the fact that we should make our decisions in harmony with God.

When we are caught in inner conflict, which movements should we follow and which should we reject? Where did this or that movement start from, and where is it leading – in the direction of love of God and neighbour, or into selfishness that is life-denying? Which path will more surely bring my heart into conformity with the heart of Christ Jesus?

GOOD AND BAD INFLUENCES

To get a perspective on what can be going on inside us, let us look back to the early Christian centuries. Some Christians who were intent on finding God went off to the deserts to do so. They noticed, however, that they had brought their baggage with them. Slowly they developed an art which they called the *discernment of spirits*. They recognised that humans are very vulnerable to temptation; the story of Adam and Eve and the temptations of Jesus illustrated it. Direct temptation to evil can be easily recognised if one's conscience is working. But here were Adam and Eve, and Jesus himself, being tempted by what appeared to be good. The belief grew, therefore, that we mere humans are under the influence of two powerful spirits – one good, the other bad. In today's terms we might say that one set of influences is supporting our efforts to live a constructive and outward-focused life, while the other is dragging us towards destructive and life-denying behaviour.

By what art, these courageous monks and hermits wondered, can we unmask the power of evil when it disguises itself under the appearance of good? How can humans, who are mainly material beings, distinguish accurately the contrary influences of good and evil that come from the *spirit-world*? Out of such pondering the *discernment of spirits* was born. The good Spirit leads us to God, but there is a dark spirit that draws us away from God, often with great subtlety. We need to notice their different styles.

Perhaps today we choose to believe only in the Holy Spirit and not in Satan. But whether or not we do, we need to identify and distinguish the influences that play upon the heart. Teilhard de Chardin in *The Divine Milieu* distinguishes the friendly and favourable forces which encourage our growth from the hostile powers that obstruct our development. Christian belief is that God is always drawing us towards the fullness of potential implanted in us. We are drawn towards love, and this will show itself in an energy and openness to life.

WHAT'S GOING ON HERE?

Earlier we spoke of the world of possibilities which we inhabit but often ignore. If we take our cues from others - parents, colleagues, culture, media - we can feel trapped within a life of dull routine. Our culture, like an anaconda, can wrap us around so tightly that it squeezes the life out of us. This leads to a malaise, a boredom and aimlessness, a wasting of potential. Yet all the time life's possibilities lie open before us. Opportunities for growth and development are all around, once we believe that we are meant to live life to the full and emerge as our true selves.

When you begin to attend to your inner world, discernment of spirits moves from theory to practice. You must, however, not become so fixated with inner observations as to forget that you are a disciple of Jesus. Your major task is to watch out for how he is leading you, even if you limp on the path. It is *within* the context of discipleship that we are to pay attention to our experiences of consolation and desolation.

WHEN I'VE BEEN HURT

The action of the differing spirits becomes crystal clear when I feel I've been hurt by a friend. My first reaction is to think of punishing them. They become my *enemy*, for the moment at least. But I may notice that this tit-for-tat approach leaves me uneasy. Why so? Because the good Spirit is trying to get my attention. Jesus' injunctions, 'Love your enemies: forgive others from your heart' may come to mind. So I have to go another way – perhaps first by calming down, then by telling the other how I have experienced what they did, and trying to negotiate a settlement. Perhaps the other person acted in innocence; perhaps I tend to take myself too seriously; perhaps I haven't accepted the fact that my friend has flaws, and that I too have plenty, so two inadequates are trying to make their way along the path of life together. I like the humorous phrase, 'Don't take yourself too seriously, because others certainly don't!'

CASE STUDY: ÓSCAR ROMERO

Óscar Romero became Archbishop of San Salvador in 1977. He was a compromise candidate, elected to head the conservative National Conference of Bishops. He was a predictable, orthodox, pious bookworm who was known to criticize those clergy who aligned with impoverished farmers seeking land reform.

But an event took place within three weeks of his election that would transform the ascetic and timid Romero. A Jesuit priest, Rutilio Grande, was ambushed and killed along with two parishioners, because he defended the peasants' rights to organise farm cooperatives. Rutilio had said that the dogs of the big landowners ate better food than the children whose fathers worked their fields.

Romero drove out of the capital to view Grande's body. In a packed country church he encountered the silent stoicism of peasants who were facing a regime of terror. Their eyes asked the question which only he could answer: 'Will you stand with us as Rutilio did?' That night he experienced the people as church and knew what he must do. 'When I looked at Rutilio lying there dead I thought, "If they have killed him for doing what he did, then I too have to walk the same path".' Poor and rich were shocked: the poor never expected him to take their side and the elites of Church and State felt betrayed. He was a surprise also to himself.

Romero begged for international intervention for his people, but it never came. He was alone. The people were alone. In 1980 the violence of the military regime claimed the lives of three thousand per month, with corpses clogging the streams, and mutilated bodies thrown in garbage dumps and the streets of the capital. With one exception, all the Salvadoran bishops turned their backs on Romero, going so far as to send a secret document to Rome, accusing him of being politicised and of seeking popularity. He refused to attend government functions until the repression of the people was stopped. He kept that promise, winning the enmity of the government and military, and an astonishing love from the poor.

He said, 'If they don't let us speak, if they kill all the priests and the bishop too, and you are left a people without priests, each one of you must become God's microphone, each one of you must become a prophet.' In one of his final homilies, he foretold his own fate: 'Christ invites us not to fear persecution because, believe me, brothers and sisters, the one who is committed to the poor must share the same fate as the poor. And in El Salvador we know the fate of the poor: to disappear, to be held captive, to be tortured, and to be found dead at the side of the road.'

On 23 March 1980, Romero openly challenged the army: 'Brothers, you are from the same people, yet you kill your fellow peasant. No soldier is obliged to obey an order that is contrary to the will of God.' There was thunderous applause; he was inviting the army to mutiny. Then he challenged its generals: 'In the name of God, in the name of this suffering people I ask you, I beg you, I command you: stop the repression.'

The next day, moments before he was murdered by the El Salvador regime as he was offering Mass, he said, 'One must not love oneself so much as to avoid getting involved in the risks that history demands of us'. A martyr for the poor, his cause for canonisation is underway.

MY COMMENTS

➢ We see that Romero was shocked into taking his stand as he stood by the body of Rutilio Grande, but we can be sure that God was working away on his heart long before that dramatic moment when he capitulated.

- He was shy, conservative, and 'a safe pair of hands'. It seemed that the status quo had nothing to fear from him. Yet God can work on a good heart. Romero was pious, and would have known from prayerful reflection on the scriptures that God is on the side of the poor, and that Jesus died to free the oppressed from all forms of domination.
- We know little of what goes on in the depths of others, but we do know from personal experience that it takes time for us to reach our deepest place where God resides. We can guess that Romero may have long been fighting an inner battle to acknowledge the truth of his country's situation.
- The promptings of his culture and his timid personality would have been at odds with the unambiguous call of Jesus in the Gospels. Inner resistance could well have held him captive for a lifetime, but a dramatic event removed the vestiges of self-delusion, and he yielded to the unwanted insights that he had repressed until then.
- His choice was born out of love for the oppressed, not out of hatred for their oppressors, so we can affirm that it was from God. He was given a new courage to speak out, despite what would happen to him. He did all he could to achieve justice by peaceful means. He never wavered from the cause of the poor. He was through and through a man of the Gospel. He discerned the contrary spirits, and, like a good money changer, he found pure gold.

YOUR COMMENTS

_____

_____

_____

_____

_____

_____

_____

_____

_____

 We need to be free of compromises, prejudices and ideologies.

HOW GOD WORKS ON OUR HEARTS

God's task is to make human hearts grow in love, and God achieves it, it seems to me, by endlessly presenting us with the needs of others. Our parents responded to our needs as infants, and this made them grow in love. Unconsciously, they were teaching us to care for the needs of others. Since we live in a world of mutual need, everyone has plenty of people to practise their love on. This is how God works: things are 'set up' for us to become people of great love. Suffering is not good: God works to take it away from us, as we see in Jesus' healing miracles. But God makes use even of suffering to break open our narrow hearts.

We can think of God orchestrating the world, playing on every heart, evoking the best in each, bringing music wherever possible. The great theologian John Calvin uses the image of a theatre – we are on the stage, and God is in the audience watching us. I prefer to think that God is like a great conductor who is signalling us to sing in harmony, even when we are out of tune.

GOD AS THE GREAT TEACHER

Ignatius uses another image: he describes God as his schoolteacher, who kept nudging him until he got the point. If you have been a teacher you know how creative you have to be to get inattentive pupils to catch on. You keep setting things up to help them – words, charts, exercises, examples, rewards and sanctions, until the penny drops and the pupils understand. Without you the pupils will not learn, and yet they are free to learn or not. God, of course, as their creator has been at work before you showed up, giving them the *capacity* to learn. There is in them some desire for knowledge, no matter how dull its flame may be. We can think of the world as God's classroom – God is the teacher and we are the pupils. The lesson is 'love', and we will be examined on it when we meet the Lord face to face, as Simon Peter did when he was asked, 'Do you love me?' God starts the lesson by loving us limitlessly. God keeps setting things up so that we can grow in love and so learn to love others.

Could it be that God works through *everything* around us, inviting us to grow in love? This would give new meaning to life! Recently I was caught by a splendid sunset. I could have missed it, but I was there and I saw it, and something good happened in me. Christian liturgy speaks of God as the One 'from whom comes all that is good'. Goodness and beauty are all around me: sometimes I notice and my heart is moved. But where do goodness and beauty come from? Do I notice their Author? Human need is all around me: sometimes I see it and choose to respond rightly. As we have seen, we live in a world brimming with possibilities. I can be in a crowd of people – on the street, at a match, in a theatre – and see none of them, or like St Francis of Assisi, I can see crowds as the image of God multiplied but not monotonous. It's my choice, my decision.

GRATITUDE

Since God is involved in every detail of life, we can ask God, 'What are you saying to me in this situation?' This is the question that springs from the discerning heart. Sometimes the answer is simple, and it centres on *gratitude*. I am invited to thank God for all that is good – a person, my health, an insight, a sunset, a job. Through all good things God reveals his love for me. As I catch on, I come to see more spontaneously that God is showering me with goodness. 'You crown the year – and me – with your goodness!' (see Psalm 65:11). I also became aware of the fact that every situation, no matter how uncomfortable, can lead me to greater love. Growth in love is the central lesson that God tries to get across to me. As the old translation of the second Eucharistic Prayer puts it, 'Make us grow in love'. This is the labour of God in our lives.

As gratitude grows, I begin to see the truth of Pope Francis' statement: 'When everything is said and done, we are infinitely loved' (*The Joy of the Gospel*, n. 6). Why should the Gospel bring us joy? Because it reveals the fact that we are limitlessly loved. Saint Paul highlights this when he says 'Christ loved me and delivered himself for me' (Galatians 2:20). This leads him on to the daring statement, 'We know that all things work together for good for those who love God' (Romans 8:28).

'WHAT ARE YOU SAYING TO ME HERE?'

A range of options may present themselves and I do not know which to choose, so I ask God to show me. On the broader level I can ask, 'What shall I do with my life?' 'What ought I do for Christ?' 'What is the Spirit saying to the Church today?' (see Revelation 2:7). In 1206 at San Damiano, God spoke to young Francis of Assisi, 'Francis, repair my Church'. Our present pope has taken the name of Francis because he recognises that God speaks again today, asking that the Church be repaired. Pope Francis is calling on all Christians to become carriers of the Good News – this is the challenge of *The Joy of the Gospel* – so I ask, 'What can I do for you, Lord?' When we open our hearts in this way, we find a gentle answer comes through a good impulse, a good idea, a book, a friend, or a request for help pinned to a Church noticeboard. If you are attuned to the inner movements of the Spirit, to where your heart is vibrating at its deepest level, then you will know where God is working in your life.

 The Spirit always sends the believer on a journey, and we are to be available to the projects of God, as collaborators in the great history of salvation.

Pope Francis

 THE HEART IN SCRIPTURE

Discernment is an affair of the heart. It is an effort to be in tune with the heart of someone I love, in this case, God.

Let us say a little more about the heart. 'Heart' is more than part of our anatomy; it refers to the mysterious core of our being, where we work things out with ourselves, take up attitudes, and make decisive choices. We judge people by the quality of their hearts. 'He has a good heart; it's in the right place'; 'That was a heartless thing to do'; 'Her heart isn't in that job'; 'She's been heartbroken since her son died'. So we use the word 'heart' to indicate what a person is truly made of, what sort they are, how they relate to others. The word 'soul' tries to point to the same capacity in us.

WHERE GOD MEETS ME

The heart is the place where Another is present to us. There God and I meet. The heart is the arena in which the relationship between God and myself is being worked out. God is always there, even if I am not, for the heart is where conscience presides. It is in the human heart, in the depths of our being, that we, like Jacob of old, wrestle with God (see Genesis 32:24), as we try to bring our wills into harmony with God's. The demands of God are radical, so the chosen people keep dodging them. 'The human heart is devious above all else: it is *perverse* – who can understand it?' (Jeremiah 17:9). They resort to external worship; but God *sees the heart* (1 Samuel 16:7) and laments that his people's heart is *far from him* (Isaiah 29:13). The people are asked to love the Lord and to seek him with *all their hearts* (Deuteronomy 4:29; 6:5) yet their history reveals their radical inability to respond. But instead of abandoning them in despair, God lures them into the wilderness and *speaks to their hearts* (Hosea 2:16). Moses and God used to meet each day in what was called 'the tent of meeting'. Presumably they discussed the affairs of the day, and Moses took God's advice. We can think of our hearts as a tent of meeting where we can make our decisions with God's help.

THE BOOK OF CHOICES

Do you ever read the Bible? I suggest that if you read it as a history of choices it comes to life. Good and bad choices collide; divine and human wills wrestle with one another on every page. Discernment is at a premium. The biblical authors exhaust themselves in a bid to get a stubborn people to listen to God and to act accordingly. But they fail. From the opening scene of Adam and Eve deciding to disobey God, to the final struggle in the Book of Revelation, readers can appreciate each choice that is made and the motivation behind it. The Bible is a drama about decision-making, good and bad. We can learn a great deal from it and identify with its characters. Take Adam and Eve: there they are, surrounded by all that is good, given high dignity, beloved by God. They are nothing less than the very images of God. But they decide to strike out for independence, to work out for themselves what is good and what is bad. So they, who should have kept God before their eyes, rupture their life-giving relationship with the divine. They hide from God. Once they lose the plot, a tragic history unfolds – murder, jealousy, disintegration of relationships, the flood. Their failure in decision-making works out in their sad history. And we know what that is like.

THE GOLDEN THREAD

There are of course exceptions. The golden thread of discernment runs through scripture, and we ourselves can follow it. Young King Solomon, who is already wise beyond his years, realises that his task of governing is beyond him, so he *prays to God* for a heart that is 'able to discern between good and evil' (1 Kings 3:9). His insight is that his people are really *God's* people, so God must know best how they should be governed. He asks God to share that knowledge with him so that he may always act rightly. Ours would be a different world if those in power today could pray like Solomon.

Young Samuel also responds to God. He prays, 'Speak, Lord, for your servant is listening' (1 Samuel 3:9-10). The psalmist also stands out as someone who 'keeps God always before his eyes' (Psalm 16:8). Psalm 119, the longest of the psalms, is an extended prayer for the gift of good judgement or discernment. Later, Wisdom literature presents the elements of discernment: 'With you is wisdom. Send her forth that she may labour at my side and that I may learn what is pleasing to you. Then my works will be acceptable' (Wisdom 9:9-11). Discernment is a gift to be asked for. It brings happiness and a blessing to the human heart, so we can be sure that God offers it generously to us.

A HEART OF FLESH

God emerges as full of compassion for his wayward people. 'A new heart I will give you, and a new spirit I will put within you; and I will remove from your body the heart of stone and give you a heart of flesh' (Ezekiel 36:26). Jesus is presented as the one who fulfils this promise: he shares his love recklessly and so brings about human conversion. Jesus is very uncompromising about the fact that real evil comes from the heart. 'Out of the heart come wicked plans, murders ...' (Matthew 15:19). To the *pure of heart* he promises the vision of God (Matthew 5:8). His own heart is pure love: on the Cross he forgives others from his heart. His words set on fire the *hearts of the disciples* on the Emmaus road (Luke 24:32). With the sending of the Holy Spirit the love of God is *poured into our hearts* (Romans 5:5), and thus we are transformed. In the widest sense, Jesus reveals how the human heart should be. The heart is the battlefield in which the world is shaped. Each good decision brings growth in love, and as we shall see later, a good heart helps to transform the world. The early

Christians were right about the need for us to know our own hearts and the opposing forces that try to guide them.

'LISTEN TO HIS VOICE TODAY!'

We could of course read the Bible and say, 'Well, that was long ago ...' But the point is that you and I are dealing with the same God as the Hebrews did. God is as concerned now as then about the oppression of people. The powerful of today ignore the contemporary prophets who denounce the injustices that ravage our world. What God wants done is dismissed as irrelevant, whether it be the call to share the world's goods, to respond to the plight of refugees or to avert the destruction of the environment. But for each of us the question arises: Do I listen? Do I see these realities as the raw material for my choices? We will deal with communal issues later, but even in our personal decision-making we are either becoming more open or more closed to the concerns of God.

Jesus takes on the role of a prophet – that is, he indicates with great clarity his Father's 'take' on human interactions. He says, 'Be loving; be forgiving; respect everyone as God does; do not sin; share with the needy; do what is right even at great cost to yourself; share the Good News.' Mercy and forgiveness are to be the atmosphere of the new world order which he inaugurates; community is to be inclusive and respectful; the goods of the world are to be shared; and there is to be no domination or superiority among God's people. There is plenty here to ponder in our decision-making!

The early Christians saw Jesus as the exemplar of how we should make our choices. They describe him as the Way, the Truth and the Life. He is the model, the archetype, of how human beings can be. They notice how totally set he is on doing what the Father wants him to do. He is the One who keeps God always before his eyes, and so his followers must learn to do likewise. His guidelines for decision-making are all God-centred. The way he lives out his life and faces his death reveals that for him the Father's will comes first. Nothing else matters.

SILENT PROPHETS?

How do you rate yourself as a prophet? Vatican II reminds us that we are to be like Christ in his prophetic role. When we see situations around us which run contrary to the spirit of the Gospels, we are to ask God what we should do about them. Once we abandon our cosy mediocrity and develop discerning hearts, we will always have plenty to grapple with.

Our Christian identity lies here. The Jesuits reminded themselves of this when recently they asked themselves, 'Who are we?' Their response was, 'We know who we are by looking at Jesus'. We are not meant to live private lives, with only occasional reference to God. We have meaning only insofar as we live for God and for what God loves. Simon Peter in the Gospels learnt this the hard way: aware of the treachery his heart was capable of when he let Jesus out of his sight, he came to understand in his lakeside encounter with the risen Jesus that for the future, everything would depend on his following close to his Lord.

Ignatian spirituality is ill at ease with half-measures. For Ignatius, *everything* is to be directed to God – he uses the word 'todo' ('all' or 'everything') almost one thousand times in his writings. This grew from his extended convalescence after injury: he fell in love with the Jesus of the Gospels, whose life and death revealed that he loved Ignatius limitlessly. Christian living and decision-making are nothing short of an extended love affair. People in love try to make their decisions in light of the preference of the other. When the disposition of my heart is to want whatever God wants, by pleasing God I please myself.

 Christian decision-making is a love affair: two hearts are in harmony, God's and mine.

# CONSOLATION

The invitation, 'Do not be afraid ... I am with you always ...' recurs often in scripture. But how is God present to us? Once you learn to acknowledge the signs of the presence of the good Spirit you become surer in your decision-making. This is what *consolation* is about.

In the introduction I explained that Christian decision-making is not a sure-fire or magical way to make perfect decisions. I acknowledged the importance of all that management literature can bring to the process of choosing well, and highlighted how Christian decision-making brings in a new dimension, the divine. Engaging God as our consultant makes the process comprehensive. Now we look at the skill of interpreting God's interventions. We look first at the inner experience of *consolation*.

At the deepest level, consolation for a Christian is an enduring joy that may be taken for granted and perhaps hardly noticed. Its origin lies in what has been done for humankind through Jesus Christ. Anxiety about the meaning of life is radically overcome, and hope emerges that death is not the end of everything but a passageway to eternal joy. There was a palpable buzz in the early Church because of the 'Good News' of human redemption. Joy and consolation are recurring themes in the New Testament writings which centre on what Jesus has won for us. With this as a foundation, we can look at the importance of attending to consolation in our decision-making.

We are made for God, and our good decisions bring us closer to God. But closeness to God brings a sense of strength, harmony, peace, courage, togetherness. We can experience these qualities when we are making our choices, and we call such indicators consolation. One option rather than the other gives us a sense of direction: we feel that we are 'on our thread', 'on the right wavelength', 'tuned in'. Consolation carries a sense of integrity and appropriateness: 'I'm together: this is me. I'm facing the right way now.' My energy is focused towards what is good and loving: I feel I can cope, even though the decision I'm making will have its difficulties. I feel I am in the light rather than floundering around in the dark. I'm like a homing pigeon, battling its way through bad weather and strong winds, until it arrives at its coop. We can grow steadily in sensitivity to consolation and check out our choices against it. It is a language that God uses and that we can learn.

CONSOLATION OF SPIRIT

God wants us to be in consolation, not in desolation or some grey area in between. But consolation is not essentially about feeling nice and comfortable, though such feelings can accompany it. It is basically about being aligned with God. It can be present as much in the wintry times of our lives as in the bright times: the wind that blows my boat to its harbour can be cold and piercing, or it can be a gentle breeze. Either will do – what matters is that I am on course, and moving towards God. Peace and harmony can often be deep down and I need to search for them beneath surface turbulence.

Karl Rahner uses the term 'wintry spirituality' to describe the state of unemotional adherence to God, where will power alone keeps us faced in the right direction, without bodily resonance. For some people in the final stages of life, the body is disintegrating, yet they are strangely patient and accepting. This is 'tough consolation'! They are set on their heart's desire, which is God. There is a sense of closeness to God that is deeper than feeling but no less real, even though they may have no words for it. Likewise, after his decision was made on the Mount of Olives, Jesus was at peace, if only at the deepest level of his being.

We are concerned here with consolation of the spirit. Spirit refers to that dimension deep within us where the Holy Spirit dwells.

When we are 'tuned in' to God we experience 'consolation of spirit' because our spirit is in harmony with God's. This experience comes, not from transient feelings or success, but ultimately from being at one with God.

Are you sometimes aware of an inner energy, harmony, peace, joy, togetherness, authenticity, love? Do you find that such states of heart are linked to what you believe to be truly good? Are you happy to name them as consolation and accept that they are indicators of being in tune with God?

Ignatius is reported to have said that he could not live without consolation. He hardly meant that he floated on clouds of euphoria – he suffered a lot of ill-health, and he refers to 'the sad misery of this life'. Rather I suggest that the Christian vision meant everything to him; if it disappeared, his life would be lived in desolation. He also meant that he could not live without the conviction that what he was engaged in was pleasing to God. Even in difficult situations he could say, 'This is tough, but I believe it is right and pleasing to God.' Here we touch on the world of desires: in the good person the deepest desire is to please God. We can grow to be at home in that fundamental desire, and so live in consolation.

THE AFTERTASTE OF EXPERIENCE

Ignatius experienced a medley of feelings on his sick bed as he dreamed of a woman he had fallen in love with, and then dreamed of following Christ and imitating the saints. He didn't invent these feelings; he noticed them only gradually, and he judged that they must be God's way of showing him that he should follow one path rather than another. God, he decided, works not only through our imaginations and our minds, but through our feelings, and uses them to nudge us to what is best. Of course, reflectiveness is needed if I am to notice the aftertaste of my experiences. Was this or that experience 'sweet or sour'?

Around the world, people who live according to their consciences are practising discernment whether they know God or not. They make their choices in line with what they believe to be truly good, and they experience a basic happiness, a sense of authenticity, of rightness, in doing so. They live in consolation though they may never name it as such. They would say that to act against their consciences would leave them in disquiet and violate what makes them truly human. Consolation is the conviction that I am doing what God wants; a quiet joy will usually accompany it.

We noted earlier how Newman followed his conscience, despite the pain involved. He suffered greatly in doing so, but he was at peace. 'From the time I became a Catholic ... I have been in perfect peace and contentment. I never have had one doubt ... It was like coming into port after a rough sea, and my happiness remains ...'

We too can develop a sensitivity, a taste, for what is right and good. The Spanish word *sentir* was used by Ignatius to convey an inner conviction that this or that is right in this situation, and that to ignore it would be to do violence to your best self and your relationship to God. *Sentir* is a feel for the language of God, which is made known to me in my heart without words. Jesus promises this consolation to his followers, despite all their difficulties (see John 16:16-33). This is the way he fulfils his promise to remain present to us.

 Every experience brings its own aftertaste, to be discovered by reflection. It helps me to chart my way forward.

CASE STUDY: THE TRAPPISTS OF ALGERIA

Our Lady still keeps watch outside an abandoned monastery in Algeria. In May 1996, six of its eight occupants, French Trappist monks, were abducted and murdered. Their story was later made into the film *Of Gods and Men*, perhaps one of the best movies ever made on Christian commitment. It also ranks as a great example of the power of humble decision-making.

An Islamic group was terrorising the little village close to the monastery. Death threats were issued to French citizens and to all foreigners. The local authorities begged the monks to leave. The monks met around their common table to discuss their options. They were ordinary people, not very different from ourselves. They got on one another's nerves, they wavered and disagreed over what to do. 'Perhaps it would be better to go home to France and serve God in a quieter way?' 'What good would our deaths bring? In a wave of violent deaths, the murder of a few monks would be nothing special.' 'No, we should stay, because God has called us here.'

The meeting ends, not with consensus, but with an agreement that each needs to pray more about what God might be asking. We witness their individual struggles, their soul-searching, their fear. The pressure of the situation throws the depth of their commitment to Jesus Christ into clear relief. Slowly, through prayer, pain, tears and mutual support, each comes to terms with himself. When next they gather at the table, one by one, each affirms that he wants to stay, come what may. And so they put themselves at total risk. These men were not heroes, they did not choose death – rather, they knew that it was coming and that they must adjust rightly to it or betray not only their Muslim neighbours, but also the silent God who was the love of their lives. They would also betray their truest selves. They have a little feast, with two bottles of good wine, a rare luxury. They drink it slowly, laugh with one another, shed tears, and gaze into the future that awaits them. The monastery was ransacked, they were taken away, held briefly as hostages, and then beheaded.

In his last testament the abbot addresses his prospective Islamic killer: 'Thank you, my friend of the last moment, who will not know what you are doing ... May we meet in heaven, like happy thieves, if it pleases God, our common Father.'

MY COMMENTS

> The silence of God in this drama is startling. God seems neither to answer prayer nor protect these good men from their fate. God waits on their individual decisions, while working in the depths of their hearts. God will work with whatever choice each one makes, in order to bring good out of it.

> Our Lady plays an unobtrusive but vital role. We are repeatedly shown the statue of the woman who said, 'Yes. Here I am, the servant of the Lord; let it be with me according to your word.'

> The monks' decision to take time to pray and reflect changes the dynamic. God is given the chance to work with each member of the community.

> The uniqueness of each man is revealed – the ambiguity of their love and commitment, the struggle to live out the discipleship each had promised. Each goes through the storms of the heart: open discussion brings hidden emotions to light. Each is revealed as needing God in unique ways.

> One by one they are given the inner freedom that enables them to say yes to their deepest desire, which is to be faithful to God. They in turn trust that God will be faithful to them.

> ➢ Companionship emerges among them: they come to a profound respect for one another and a mutual acceptance of the mystery of human life and death. God is silently at work, building community and bringing good to others across the world through this dreadful situation.

YOUR COMMENTS

 It is in making serious decisions that we come to know our own hearts, and our need of God.

 # DESOLATION

Consider the antithesis of consolation and you have desolation: a profound sense of uneasiness and despair.

> Desolation is a movement of the spirit in a direction away from God ... Desolation moves inward. It gets trapped in the self. It likes privacy ... Desolation is confused, in the dark, in twilight, in avoidance. It is dispersed; its single focus has been lost. It wriggles so that it can escape facing reality. The mechanisms of avoidance include escape into words and analysis. Avoidance will do anything so as not to make a decision. It marks time. It postpones the pain of giving up, of giving in. It clings to the dull discomfort of its condition, rather than facing the sharp pain that may liberate it into peace ... It feels that there is no point to doing anything. It is good at masking torpor with an energetic semblance of vitality, with business. It is busy about good works, (but only as) an effective cushion between the (human) spirit and God.
>
> Joseph Veale, *Manifold Gifts*

LET'S EXPLORE THAT DESCRIPTION OF DESOLATION

One comes across people who strangely lack 'soul'. They may be well-to-do, well educated, respectable. They work hard looking after their affairs and their families. They are self-sufficient; they neither depend on others, nor do they allow others to depend on them. They try to be buoyant and imperturbable, but have limited horizons within which to interpret the painful side of life. In cocktail chatter they lament the failings of society and government, but they avoid getting engaged. They exclude themselves from the world of the poor. They keep busy, tick all the right boxes, do no harm. They take care of their appearances, enjoy holidays in exotic places, and are 'comfortable'.

But somehow they are less than fully alive. They have set their own boundaries, so that 'real life' cannot get at them. They endure an unspoken emptiness. They are not happy. They are among the many who, in Thoreau's phrase, live lives of quiet desperation. If they believe in an afterlife at all, they would want to live more or less as here on earth, within their own comfort zone, and at a safe distance from others. They would think of themselves as being in consolation, but how deep does it go?

The Latin word for 'sun' is 'sol'. So it helps me to think that *con-sol-ation* means 'being in the sun'. Its light and warmth brings growth and fruitfulness. 'De-sol-ation' means 'being without the sun', or being trapped in a dark cave where things cannot grow.

Desolation is the contrary to consolation. When you are desolate, the world becomes narrow and more constraining. You imagine that God is absent. You are out of sorts, off-key, off-centre, you are in a spin, fragmented and moody, preoccupied with inner struggles, missing out on joy, seeing things as grey or black. You feel unsure, unhappy, separated and lonely; you tend to put bad interpretations on what others say or do. You lose courage and your judgements can be unbalanced and negative. In desolation your personal demons are hard at work, drawing you away from God, whereas in consolation the good Spirit is leading you towards God, even if the journey is along a stony path.

At the end of one of his letters, Ignatius prays 'that our weak, sad spirits may be transformed and become strong and joyful in his praise' (*Writings*, 117). He wants God to rescue us from desolation, so that we may live in the strength and joy of consolation. This is exactly what God wishes for us. For the colour of our lives, we can choose between a rainbow and a grey sky.

CORRECTING THE TAIL-SPIN

Discernment is needed to get out of the bondage of desolation, and it can take the best part of a lifetime. When we attain some personal enlightenment it hits us that we were mostly making choices that were well-intentioned, but we were choosing also to ignore warning signs that we were going about things the wrong way. I mentioned earlier my overdue insight into my style of proceeding – the realisation that 'it's all been a great mistake!' Poor choices bring desolation into our lives, but we can become so accustomed to 'not being at our best' that we take the grey colours of desolation as the norm.

Why can it take some of us years or even decades to attain the insights we need to help us to live lovingly and respect others in their differences? We can pick up a flawed understanding of life early on. Family culture and society present us with an inadequate set of values. Imagine yourself as a child growing up in the apartheid regime in South Africa. As a white child you would have diligently imitated your parents and accepted their biases as normal. So you are building your life on a warped foundation and breathing in a polluted atmosphere. Insights that would challenge your inherited values are rejected because they are alien; they would shake up your whole world and set you on a collision course with your family. So your life project gets distorted, and this brings on desolation because you are not becoming your true self.

On a more personal level, you may notice that you are out of sorts, and wonder why. If you reflect, it may come to you that you are withholding forgiveness from someone who has wronged you, and that you need to change on this. Desolation can contain hidden energy which nags us to do something to return to a more loving way of life. In this sense it is not simply bad.

ATTENDING TO DESOLATION

Desolation can afflict cultures as well as individuals, and we can all get caught up in it. We can know well that something is wrong, but we ignore the warning signs, the flagrant injustices, all in the name of national security or 'the common good'. Therefore personal conversion can take a long time, involve much inner turmoil, and carry huge risks. It is a dangerous thing to become counter-cultural, and to speak out for Gospel values. We see what happened to Jesus who walked this particular path.

In this arena of personal conversion, it is only by attending to my experiences of desolation that I can make progress. God helps me to make the necessary changes. I may feel isolated, but I am 'the beloved of God' (Romans 1:7), so God supports me in the long journey from the false consolation which dominant groups enjoy, to the true consolation which flows from acting with God to build a community of equals. But the path winds through the desert of desolation.

 From being weak and sad, may we become strong and joyful.

St Ignatius

KEEPING GOD BEFORE YOUR EYES

We have seen that a key factor in coming to good decisions is the ability to notice the influences at play in our inner world. Only when we notice these dynamics can we control them and reach freedom. We need always ask, 'What is moving me to make this choice or its opposite? Are my motivations authentic?'

We have an innate dynamic orientation to what is good. God goes to a lot of trouble to enable us to make our way through the complexities of life. God provides us with helpful influences: good upbringings and examples; good teaching; good relationships; the goodness embedded in our culture, in our faith, in the Christian community. But other forces are also active: the ambiguity of the culture in which we live; our inclination to selfishness; wayward instincts; sinfulness; defects of character; the compulsions and evasions of our personality types.

If you were to follow your impulses your life would be chaotic. If you were to follow the crowd you would never become an integrated person. If you were always to look to others for guidance you would never become a responsible, self-sufficient adult. If you were to live by hard and fast rules you would become inflexible. But if none of these paths will help you, what can you do?

YOUR SAT NAV

In the Introduction, we noted St Ignatius' cryptic advice: 'Keep your eyes on God; then you will make good choices.' God can be for you what the cardinal point north is to an explorer using a compass. You need an inner compass, a Sat Nav (satellite navigator) to guide you to what is best. When Sat Navs first appeared on the market, they were fallible enough, but have now become more accurate. How accurate is your inner Sat Nav? It needs to be able to register where God is. This Sat Nav is your heart, and its task is to register the drawing of God. God draws you through the good influences that operate in and around you. What we call 'consolation' is an inner noticing that you are being led by God in one direction rather than another. The heart is that deep place in you from which decisions emerge, and God is active there, drawing you to what is best for you. God is always setting things up so that you can grow to the fullness of your potential. God endlessly nudges your heart towards what is good.

The language of the heart, we have said, is also the language of God. The heart accommodates a riotous mix of feelings and emotions. However, in the depth of the human heart God lives and guides us. Thomas Merton expresses a fundamental Christian insight:

> At the centre of our being is a point of nothingness, which is untouched by sin and by illusion, a point of pure truth, a point or spark which belongs entirely to God, which is never at our disposal, from which God disposes of our lives, which is inaccessible to the fantasies of our own mind or the brutalities of our own will. This little point of nothingness and of absolute poverty is the pure glory of God in us. It is so to speak his name written in us, as our poverty, as our indigence, as our dependence, as our sonship and daughterhood. It is like a pure diamond, blazing with the invisible light of heaven. It is in everybody.

Thomas Merton, *Conjectures of a Guilty Bystander*
(Image, 1968)

God is the Mysterious Other who is also amazingly close, and dwells inside us. Jesus promises this: 'Those who love me keep my word, and my Father will love them, and we will come to them and make our home with them' (John 14:23). When the divine Persons make their home in us they don't sit in their room quietly watching the television: they engage with us at the table, chat with us in the evenings and suggest ideas around whatever is going on! As we grow in inner freedom, we can sense the action of God more easily. We have noted Ignatius' image of the soul being like a weighing scales at equilibrium (Exercises 15). God can gently touch one or other side of the scale to indicate how best to choose.

THE DISCERNING HEART

There follows from this the fact that while personal discernment deals with particular options and concrete choices, it is not to be just an occasional practice. Its wider goal is *a discerning heart*. Solomon's prayer is for a discerning heart, not simply for the capacity to make right judgements as required (1 Kings 3:9). A discerning heart is always on the alert; it is a listening heart. 'Speak, Lord, your servant is listening' (1 Samuel 3:10). Mary's prayer was not a once-off event when she responded to the angel: 'Let it be done to me according to your word' (Luke 1:38). In the struggle for conversion Paul asked: 'What shall I do, Lord?' and this became his prayer for the remainder of his life (Acts 22:10). The discerning heart is the sensitive orientation of one's whole being toward God, so that like Jesus we can come to say, 'I always do what pleases God' (John 8:29). This is a radical placing of myself at God's disposal, the opposite of the stance of Adam and Eve who say, 'We'll decide for ourselves!' (see Genesis 3:1-6).

This stance of openness to God can make great demands. I may be deeply attached to one option rather than another, as was Jesus in Gethsemane. Discerning in such a situation is not a 'happy-feely' experience. It may demand blood, sweat and tears, as Jesus found (see Luke 22:44). My feelings and emotions may rebel against a decision made in deep faith; the process of integrating conviction and emotions can be slow. Although consolation gives a sense of authenticity in the core of my being, this may have a hard time welling through to my pores. This is where noticing is again important. When you make a conscientious decision to emigrate, or to move away from a partner with whom you have shared your life, your heart may well be breaking. Consolation will be hardly perceptible, and yet you believe, rather than feel, that the decision is the best one you can make under the circumstances. Consolation expresses outward-bound love, while desolation leads into a downward spiral of emptiness.

THE COOK

Saint Ignatius' formula, 'keep God before your eyes' is not original. It echoes the scripture line, 'As the eyes of servants look to the hand of their master, as the eyes of a maid to the hands of her mistress, so our eyes look to the Lord our God' (Psalm 123:2). Psalm 145:15 is perhaps a bit optimistic in asserting that, 'The eyes of all look to you' – this is more an aspiration than a reality. In fact, things are usually the other way round; often God is trying to catch my eye while I am looking elsewhere.

Ignatius uses the humble image of a cook to show the importance of 'catching God's eye' before making a decision. The cook is wondering what his master wants for dinner. No amount of discussion with the kitchen staff will decide the issue. The master's desire can be ascertained only by asking him what his preference might be. We can imagine the cook tramping upstairs, fish in one dish and beef in the other. He stands before the master, but it won't do for him to keep his eyes on his plates. He needs to keep his eyes on the master to notice which plate gets the nod.

Keeping God before your eyes is a receptive or contemplative stance. But it is geared to action. Once you get the nod you are to hurry off to do what you believe God wants done. This attitude can be termed a 'mysticism of service'. Many Christians have it, though they would be surprised to find themselves called 'servant mystics' or 'contemplatives in action'. But they love God and want to please God. 'God, help me to choose rightly.' may be their simple prayer, as they reflect on their experiences in the course of a day. Faith for them is more than an assent to divine truth: it is a radical aligning of their lives with the values of Jesus.

 You hold my right hand, you guide me with your counsel.

Psalm 73:23-24

CASE STUDY: SOLOMON

We have mentioned Solomon's prayer for wisdom, and how it worked out in one dramatic case. Solomon lived some three thousand years ago, but his story can still touch our hearts. (see 1 Kings 3:3-28).

> Solomon loved the Lord, walking in the statutes of his father David. Only, he sacrificed and offered incense at pagan shrines. The Lord appeared to him in a dream by night; and said, 'Ask what I should give you.'
>
> And Solomon said, 'O Lord my God, you have made your servant king in place of my father David, although I am only a little child; I do not know how to go out or come in. And your servant is in the midst of the people whom you have chosen, a great people. Give your servant therefore an understanding mind to govern your people, able to discern between good and evil.'
>
> It pleased the Lord that Solomon had asked this. God said to him, 'Because you have asked this, and have not asked for yourself long life or riches, or for the life of your enemies, but have asked for yourself understanding to discern what is right, I now do according to your word. Indeed I give you a wise and discerning mind; no one like you has been before you and no one like you shall arise after you. I give you also what you have not asked, both riches and honour all your life; no other king shall compare with you. If you will walk in my ways, as your father David walked, then I will lengthen your life.'
>
> Then Solomon awoke; it had been a dream. He came to Jerusalem, where he stood before the ark of the covenant of the Lord. He offered up burnt-offerings and offerings of well-being, and provided a feast for all his servants.
>
> Later, two women came to the king. One woman said, 'Please, my lord, this woman and I live in the same house; and

we both gave birth. Then this woman's son died in the night, and she took my son from beside me while I slept. She laid her dead son at my breast. When I rose in the morning to nurse my son, I saw that he was dead; but when I looked at him closely, clearly it was not the son I had borne.' But the other woman said, 'No, the living son is mine, and the dead son is yours.' The first said, 'No, the dead son is yours, and the living son is mine.' So they argued before the king. So Solomon said, 'Bring me a sword', and they brought a sword. The king said, 'Divide the living boy in two; then give half to one, and half to the other.' But the woman whose son was alive said to the king – because compassion for her son burned within her – 'Please, my lord, give her the living boy; certainly do not kill him!' The other said, 'It shall be neither mine nor yours; divide it.' Then the king responded: 'Give the first woman the living boy; do not kill him. She is his mother.' All Israel heard of the judgement that the king had rendered; and they stood in awe of the king, because they perceived that the wisdom of God was in him, to execute justice.

MY COMMENTS

➤ We may note again that dreams are not to be despised. They are one of innumerable ways through which God takes initiative in our lives.

➤ Solomon loves the Lord, so he is starting in the right place. He does not yet fully appreciate the fact that God is the only God, but that wisdom will come later. For a young man he has a high level of self-knowledge because he is aware of his inadequacy for the task God has given him.

➤ He sees himself as God's servant. He speaks directly and innocently to God, and humbly asks God to direct his life. His is a pure prayer, and God commends him for it.

➤ Like Solomon, we have God-given tasks, and we often feel inadequate in fulfilling them. It is good to speak about them with God, and to ask for what we need so that we can act justly. Solomon trusts God, and so can we. The Spirit of Wisdom is promised and given to us as it was to him. And God, who is generous, gives us gifts for which we have not asked.

➤ The gift Solomon received was a discerning mind and heart. It is this gift that enables him to read the hearts of the two women and the baby. We need this gift!

YOUR COMMENTS

 God is most at home in a discerning heart.

# LOVE OF ANOTHER KIND

WORKING WITH THE DYING

The story of Solomon belongs to another world than ours, yet his dream, his conviction and his prayer can awaken parallels in us. Ann, a colleague of mine, had to leave our employment when her job folded up. She needed an income, applied for the directorship of Retreats for Youth and was offered the post. She accepted it but immediately felt a loss of energy and enthusiasm. She prayed, talked with a good friend, and consulted her family who said that the new job was a backward step for her. She should, they said, hold out for something else; but no one had an idea what that 'something else' might look like.

Ann settled down to wait, and to pray. Slowly there emerged for her a memory and a dream which grew richer as she gave them space. While working with us, she had spent long evening hours with another member of staff who was dying of cancer. 'That's where I want to be!' she said. She felt her energy flooding back again, was accepted for a course in Chaplaincy Training, and will soon be looking out for opportunities to work with the dying.

When I am making choices, I am not alone. God is at my side, helping me. I am important to God, and my choices are important too. Let us look now at the nature of God's love for us. The surer we are about it, the easier it will be for us to take the trouble to try to find God in our choices.

A RICHER LOVE

Through the Incarnation a new love becomes known on our earth. It was not known before, so it is not to be domesticated or reduced to what went before, or boxed into narrow human boundaries. Jesus brings to us love of another kind. His dying and Resurrection best reveal the characteristics of this new love, which is so much richer than any other love we know.

> *We are loved unconditionally.* There are no terms and conditions, no ifs and buts about this new love. It is simply itself, given to us. It does not come to an end (1 Corinthians 13:8).
> *We are loved with a committed love.* This love is not swayed by emotion, nor dependent on the response it receives. God is determined, never wavering in loving us. I have already quoted Pope Francis' assertion that: 'When everything is said and done, we are infinitely loved.' 'Infinitely' means what it says!
> *We are loved with a liberating love.* Our freedom, which we treasure so deeply, is liberated from the bondage of compulsions and evasions, and can now serve us to realise our full human potential.
> *We are loved with an indiscriminate, prodigal, unmeasured love.* It is free for all. It desires everyone to be embraced by it. Imagine a huge department store opening wide its doors with the announcement, 'We have all that you need! Everything is free, and supplies are unlimited. So come on in!' God's love is like that.
> *We are loved with an endlessly forgiving love.* God's love does not hold our offences against us, but wipes the slate clean over and over - in other words, endlessly.
> *We are loved with unalloyed love.* It is simply as it says on the package. 'As the Father has loved me, so I have loved you; abide in my love' (John 15:9). This love holds no hatred, no recrimination, no harsh justice, no hostility.
> *We are loved with an endlessly active love.* That love searches us out no matter where we have strayed, no matter how hardened our hearts. It is tough, durable and determined, and it gets its way in the end.

> *We are loved with costly love.* It is best revealed in the Passion of Jesus, who gave his life for us in a brutal and violent death. This action, more than any other divine action, shows just how far this love will go to win us over.

HEALING GRACE

The new love that has unexpectedly come into our world is nothing less than a healing grace. It is the divine response to sin and evil. Despite the sinfulness of humankind, we are all swept up into this love, and are being transformed by it. No matter what problems we face, we can be radically happy about ourselves because we are so loved.

There have been many interpretations of the doctrine of original sin: one suggestion is that it refers to our deep-seated inability to believe that we are totally loved by God. 'It just can't be true that God loves me so! Why would God love the likes of me? I'm not worthy of such love.' But it so happens that God is just like that. God loves us, simply, innocently, unreservedly, the way the sun shines and the rain falls on all of us, good and bad. The worst we could do is to limit God to our all-too-human modes of loving.

AGAPE-LOVE

The early Christians were so taken by the uniqueness of the love shown in Jesus Christ that they named it 'agape-love' to distinguish it from all the other forms of love with which we are familiar. God encompasses us already in this love: God *is* this agape-love. It is in this love that our lives in all their details are played out.

When people are in love, they try to please one another. Since God is in love with us, God tries to please us. When we catch on to this remarkable fact, we try to please God in return. True discernment is born of this love. Jesus gives an example of this. He says, as a summary of his life's orientation, 'The one who has sent me is with me; he has not left me alone, for I always do what is pleasing to him' (John 8:29). So the radical question in decision-making is: 'Dear God, what would you like me to do?' Saint Ignatius tries to get this point across by saying that the love that moves me in my decision-making must come down from above, that is, it must flow from God's own love.

Let us look at how this love can affect the choices we make:
> Because we are so well loved, it is not strange that in return we should want to 'love God with all our heart and soul and mind' (Matthew 22:37). This desire will reveal itself in our decisions. We will try to love those around us, because God asks this of us and already loves them with agape-love. This new divine standard of loving is to replace our all-too-human habit of loving only those who are nice to us. Agape-love is simply different. It is divine, so our best ideas of love will only hint at it, no more.
> When we are threatened by black moods because of the behaviour of others, we need to keep our eye on Jesus as he shows agape-love in concrete forms – healing, forgiving, reaching out, respecting others, being patient. Agape-loving creates a huge challenge in regard to our 'enemies'. It accepts us when we are at our most loveless: it is unconditional, all-inclusive, gratuitous, generous, committed, forgiving, determined, undeterred by rejection. So our attitude to those we dislike must become the same.
> As the divine response to sin and evil, this love enables us to be agents of reconciliation in a fractured world. God's project in the world is all about developing good relationships. Entrusted with this love, we are now enabled to help mend the human community. We are ambassadors for Christ (2 Corinthians 5:20), and agape-love is the message we carry. Great-hearted persons like Nelson Mandela reveal it. He said, 'As I walked out the door toward the gate that would lead to my freedom, I knew if I didn't leave my bitterness and hatred behind, I'd still be in prison.'
> Once we are convinced that we are limitlessly and endlessly

loved, we worry less about our personal salvation. Instead we focus our released energy toward sharing agape-love with others in the here and now. Jesus reminds us that we are to be 'salt of the earth and light for the world' (Matthew 5:13-14).The reversal of the downward spiral of human history will be achieved insofar as this love becomes flesh in human lives. Agape-love, and nothing else, is the dynamic of the Final Community of Love which God intends. Its green shoots should already be evident in our lives.

➤ To develop a discerning heart is to adopt a radical stance, whereby we live out life in partnership with God; we try to make choices which are in harmony with God's desires and with the demands of agape-love.

 In good decision-making, agape-love irradiates the situation, and people notice!

THE SHAPING OF MY LIFE (I)

We are a species capable of extraordinary adaptation. We develop as we come to see and accept ourselves in new ways. So we make the transition from infanthood to childhood to adolescence to adulthood: then we perhaps try to settle down and build a stable world around ourselves. But things keep happening that destabilise us; our life situation changes, things do not work out as we hoped; health diminishes with the ageing process, and we slip back perhaps into second childhood until eventually death swallows us up. Should we then think of ourselves as always in process, never static but provisional, open to revision? What we have in mind for ourselves is one thing; but what reality – or God – has in mind for us may be quite another. This brings us to consider our choices again, but in a new context.

If with each change my predecessors had asked 'Who am I? What am I becoming?' their answers would have been different. But perhaps, like ourselves, they were too tired or too busy to ask such questions. Can we take some time to address our two questions today and get an overall perspective on ourselves, so that we can make appropriate choices?

BUSY ABOUT MANY THINGS

We are taken up with many things. Perhaps we feel like hamsters, racing along on our wheel, getting nowhere. Our hearts are filled with desires, needs, worries. Choices crowd in on us and we bumble our way along without any steady direction or pattern. Life can appear as a set of brute facts. We may feel that we alone are responsible for our lives and that God leaves us to ourselves. But is it so? It is liberating to become sensitive to the fact that, behind the scenes, God is busily orchestrating our lives and in all things is working for our good? When we comprehend this, we can make sense of our situation. We can then choose to say yes to what happens – to the demands of life, to suffering, illness, love and happiness. We can also choose to put a positive interpretation on 'the things we cannot change' and our choice is helped by having a sense that God is labouring in them for our good.

Try for a moment to get a handle on what's going on in your life. It's not easy! But in *The Divine Milieu*, Teilhard de Chardin makes a helpful division: he divides life's events into two categories, which he calls *activities* and *passivities* – the things I do myself, and then the things that seem just to happen to me, over which I have little or no control.

OUR ACHIEVEMENTS

Let us begin with our activities, our achievements - what we achieve in life, in sport, in business, in learning, in social life, in politics, in our efforts to build a better world. Such activities constitute the major part of our lives, since we are by nature active beings. They are the stuff of biography and autobiography. In the Genesis story humankind is given stewardship over God's creation (Genesis 1:26). Such stewardship demands innumerable decisions on our part. But where is God in them – an absentee landlord, a sleeping partner? Perhaps I have been accustomed to proceed as if my choices were mine alone. I was a founding member of a Gaelic football club in the fifties: when we passed the age of winning matches we decided to meet annually for a celebratory Mass and a party. We still meet, and everyone has a party piece. One member sings 'My Way' and he puts such energy into it that you know the sentiment clearly rings true for him. Perhaps it's true for all of us: my choice of career, of life-partner, of the size of my family, of lifestyle ... perhaps all these are *my* choices. But if I am trying to develop a discerning heart I need to go about my choices in partnership with God rather than independently.

But even granting that I want to let God in on my choice-making, how far will I let that happen? I notice personally how I waver in this area:

> ➢ I have an underlying desire to do what is right. Theologians would say that most of us have – at least implicitly – made a *fundamental option for God.*
> ➢ But sometimes I just do my own thing without any specific reference to God. I don't even *think* to consult God.
> ➢ At other times I ask God to help me do what *I have decided to do anyway.* I let God in on my decision *after* I have made it.
> ➢ As I get older, sometimes at least, I ask, 'Lord, don't let me spoil things on you.'
> ➢ And sometimes – too rarely – I say, 'Lord, what do you want me to do? Whatever it be, let me do it graciously.'

Ask yourself which of these categories define your decision-making.

SERVICE

The New Testament has two significant things to say about our life choices. First, the service of others is commanded by Jesus: he reveals by his life that God is a serving God, so we must imitate him in our service. We are to 'put our gifts at the service of others' (1 Peter 4:10). Service, then, must be a fundamental criterion in our decision-making. God sets us up for the service of others, whether we like it or not. The bus driver, the consultant, the chef, the shopkeeper, the broker, the pastor, the secretary, the parent, the teacher, the administrator – all are in different dimensions of service. We live in a world of mutual service, even if we see this only when a strike occurs. Think of the forms of service you yourself provide. And notice that you can *make the choice* to serve. It may well be that your job is dull and monotonous, perhaps the only job you could find. But there it is; it is a service to others, and that is good. To see it this way brings at least a glimmer of joy to the daily grind. You are in tune with God's intention when you serve others. When de Chardin speaks of the 'divinising' of our activities he means that they are to be irradiated by love or else they have no place in the final order of things, the Kingdom of God, the final community of Love.

LOVING SERVICE

The second thing the New Testament requires of us is that our service be *loving*. God serves us endlessly, and that service is born of love. Ours must be the same. Saint Paul puts it dramatically when he says that we could be doing good and even heroic things, and doing them 'right', but if we do them without love, they are useless (1 Corinthians 13:1–3). Love must shine through my service of others. If it is already implicitly present, well and good, but it will have a better quality when I allow it to bubble up to the surface. I spent some time in one particular community and we had one simple rule: if you were going to be in a bad mood when doing the cooking, better not to do it at all. When I cook for my community, or drive someone to the hospital and wait two hours to bring them home again, I can view such activities as chores or as acts of love. Am I thinking that I'd prefer to be doing something else, like getting on with 'my life' and with my preferred way of spending 'my time'? Or do I choose to believe that this is what God wants of me now, and can I smile back at God while doing them? There are subtle choices here, as we saw earlier when dealing with our world of possibilities.

REFLECTING BACK

It is worthwhile to look back on a period of your life, and to notice which decisions you made in partnership with God, and which were unilateral choices on your part. Were you in most situations trying to be in harmony with divine planning? Or did you waste precious time and talent in simply doing your own thing? Joseph Campbell speaks of the horror of spending a lifetime struggling to get to the top of a wall, only to discover that it was the *wrong* wall. Jesus speaks of the rich fool who missed the point of living. He stored up treasure for himself but without sparing a thought for what God might have in mind (see Luke 12:16-21).

This reflection demands discernment, for God has been orchestrating everything in my life so that I may grow in love. The divinising of my activities means that what I do is to fit into the divine scheme of things. It can be a source of wonder to look back on one's humdrum and ordinary life, and to notice that its innumerable details are contributing to the final scheme of things. This can bring us a sense of wonder and gratitude, that a lifetime of unremarkable and unremembered service is remembered by Someone Else, and is treasured and carefully crafted into the 'new Jerusalem' that is under construction (see Revelation 21).

 The innumerable details of an authentic life contribute to the beauty that will shine out in the final scheme of things.

 THE SHAPING OF MY LIFE (II)

'LOOK WHAT HAPPENED TO ME!'

I reflected in the previous section on where God is to be found in our *activities* and how we can choose to shape them into 'something beautiful for God' as Mother Teresa puts it. One of our illusions, however, is that our activities constitute the only area for our discernment. But as we age we become aware that things are happening to us over which we have little control. If we consider this awareness, we get to see that vast areas of our lives were set up for us, whether by others or by God. We have noted this earlier; now we deal with it from another point of view. I can remember coming to realise with astonishment that the things that *have happened to me* far outweigh my activities. These things that just 'happen' include the friendly and favourable influences that helped me to grow and develop. But they also include the influences that bring about my decline or diminishment (*Divine Milieu*, 19-47).

A: THE GOOD THINGS THAT SHAPED ME

Let me look back for a few moments, firstly at the *good things* that came my way without my choice. As I engage with them I begin to feel a sense of wonder – the wonder that God was there all the time, setting up my life in this world, providing what would be good for me, enabling me to engage in the riot of activities that constituted my life thus far.

So, what about me? I did not choose to exist: my life was given to me. I didn't choose to be male, white, Irish, with particular characteristics that separate me from everyone else. Innumerable favourable influences were required for my development. I didn't choose my parents, nor my place in the family, nor to be born at a particular time, nor my physical characteristics, nor my abilities and gifts. I did not choose that the country in which I was born should be neutral in World War II. Had I been born to Jewish parents in Europe, or to British parents in London, I might not have survived. I didn't choose the social and economic levels in which I grew up. My parents sacrificed a great deal for me, but all I contributed to that was *my need* – of nourishment, safety, shelter, health and education. I didn't choose the education available at that time: my parents and the Christian Brothers saw to that. Had my parents separated, or died and left me an orphan, my life would have been very different.

THE DIVINE MILIEU

Year by year, as I was learning to shape what I call 'my life' there were pre-existing supports to enable this to happen. Mother Earth has served me well: air, food, drink, light, materials – all have been given. I entered human history at a moment not of my choosing, when the human race had reached a high state of development, but I had no hand in that. Much less did I have a part in the history of human salvation which now encompasses me. I got caught up in Christianity only because my parents were Catholics. Moreover, if St Ignatius had not founded the Jesuits, I would have had to do something very different with my life. But even what I call *my* vocation to join the Jesuits came not from myself but from the Lord. 'You did not choose me, Brian: no, I chose you!' (see John 15:16). I have been living as an honoured guest in the home of Another, and well looked after too. The divine milieu was so close that it was out of my focus. Now I can take time to notice and to give thanks for all the good things I have received.

REFLECTION

So much for the good things that befell me without my choice. They are graced and blessed. The favourable chances which have enabled me to survive and to come thus far are countless. Against so many odds, here I am, shaped by Another, and shielded from so much that would have done me harm. These good influences emerged from the wise choices of others, both divine and human. They now lead me to the mystery of God, to a sensitivity that divine providence is always at work, quietly and unobtrusively, on my behalf. Then, as Gerard Manley Hopkins writes in 'The Wreck of the Deutschland', 'I greet him the days I meet him and bless when I understand'. It is God whom I meet, God who enables me to participate in divine life. de Chardin uses the imagery of hands to catch the point:

> I encounter, and kiss, your two marvellous hands – the one which holds us so firmly that it is merged, in us, with the sources of life, and the other whose embrace is so wide that, at its slightest pressure, all the springs of the universe respond harmoniously together.
>
> *Divine Milieu*, 57

WONDER AND AWE

I do not have to look far for God: God is the author of my history. God is nearer to me than I can imagine, 'closer to me than I am to myself' as Augustine says. When I look for material to pray over and contemplate, it is already here, waiting for me, in the history of my being. With a discerning heart I can review this vast dimension of my reality and choose to notice God in it. I can trace back how carefully I have been loved. God was there all the time, setting me up for life in this world, providing what would be good for me. Someone Else was doing the choosing. 'From God comes all that is good,' the liturgy explains. Hidden in what seemed accidental, chaotic, haphazard, God is the golden thread of possibility and goodness and meaning. So I come to know myself as I truly am – the beloved of God. In God I have 'lived and moved and had my being' (see Acts 17:28), and now I know it for the first time.

GOD EVER-PRESENT

'Look what's happened to me!' Here the work of discernment and of finding God in all things come together. I can find myself waking up, like Jacob of old, and exclaiming that God was in this place and that event, but I did not know it (see Genesis 28:16-17). I can pray that God may find me open and receptive to all that is yet to come. This is the stance of the discerning heart. It is full of gratitude and trust, trust that God 'whose power is at work in me is able to accomplish abundantly far more than I can ask or imagine' (see Ephesians 3:20). I pray that I may not place obstacles in God's way. This prayer is important because we have little idea what God would like to achieve in us. Ignatius spoke of himself as being nothing but an obstacle to grace, because he so often failed to attend to the divine promptings in his heart.

B: THE THINGS THAT DIMINISH ME

From considering the good things that happen to us we move on to the things that diminish us. These diminishing factors – a vast array – come both from outside and inside. From 'outside' come accidents, tragedies, misfortunes, betrayals, failures, losses and frustrations. Add in the decisions of others which may impact negatively on us. From 'inside' come our innate failings and weaknesses, physical and psychological illnesses, inability to cope. All of these limit the field of our possibilities. And even if we escape significant misfortunes, the ageing process nibbles away at our effective freedom. Finally, death, as Teilhard de Chardin says, is 'the sum and consummation of all our diminishments' (*Divine Milieu*, 61). If ageing is nature's way of telling us to slow up, death is nature's way of telling us to get off the stage!

SLOWING DOWN

The factors that bring about our diminishment exist in embryo form from the beginning. In earlier stages we try to overcome them or ignore them, or we believe we can retrieve what they take from us.

In the later stages of life – if we survive that far! – they can preoccupy us intensely. When we realise we are 'not the people we used to be', we begin to leave certain interests and pursuits behind – or rather, these are quietly taken from us. So for me, heart problems began some years ago, which meant that I could no longer climb the mountains I love. So I climbed hills for a while, but more recently I lowered my sights and adjusted to taking walks 'in the hills' but on the flat. These walks are shorter now, but they take the same amount of time! Later on I expect I will simply park and contemplate the wild beauty around me. Further on again, I will get to the hills only if some kind soul drives me and then pushes the wheelchair! Diminishment can be gentle in this way, or shocking as when one gets a stroke.

GOD TAKES OVER

Is God present in such diminishment? Is everything crumbling to dust, or in this gradual loss of life am I being set up to find the Source of Life itself? Here is where discernment has a critical role.

The first choice is to *decide* to *notice* what is going on. Ageing is an awesome and frightening task. However I am not alone: God in a real sense is closer to me now than ever before. Nobody else may be able to help me, but God is still with me. I am being lured into the desert where God will speak tenderly to me (see Hosea 2:14). My diminishment leaves God greater space to take over and become the Main Person in my life. For much of my life I may have been like an actor with a minor part who tries to dominate the stage, although I knew little more than the outline of the script and made a mess of the plot! I may have consigned God to the audience, accepting only the occasional prompt when stuck. In my later years things can change significantly. Now God and I are alone on stage. It is a grace that God should become my main concern now, but again, it is my choice to accept or ignore God's presence.

In the final stage of life, God and I are alone on stage: I take my cues from him.

 **HOLLOWED OUT**

GOD MAKING ROOM

The emptiness of later years may become filled with regrets, especially around hurts given or received. Perhaps rifts in relationships need to be addressed insofar as it is possible to do so. What we did, and what we failed to do, can be entrusted into divine hands and commended to God's creative mercy. Our prayer can be simply, 'What I did badly, God, please turn to good'. That, after all, is the characteristic work of God, to bring good out of what was bad. But again I have to choose to believe that God can transform everything. Christian tradition speaks of the 'happy fault' of Adam which occasioned great good for the world. It revealed, as nothing else could have done, the limitlessness of divine loving.

> God must, in some way or other, make room for himself,
> hollowing us out and emptying us, if he is finally to penetrate
> into us ... to re-cast and re-model us ... It [death] will put us
> into the state needed if the divine fire is to descend upon us.
> *Divine Milieu*, 68-69

Being hollowed out can be severe, but we are warned to be ready for it. In his brief years of ministry, Jesus is portrayed as active – preaching, healing, arguing, performing miracles, training his disciples. But when the Synoptic writers come to his final hours, they portray him as passive. His hollowing out is under way. Everything that happens is being done to him by others. 'They took him, they *scourged him*, they *crucified him*, they *pierced him* with a spear, they *buried him* and they *rolled a stone across the face of the tomb*.' Saint Paul emphasises Jesus' personal choice to allow all this; he says that

Jesus emptied himself or hollowed himself out. When we wonder if there is any value in the humiliating diminishments we or those we love endure, we are offered the choice to believe that suffering, 'the divine fire' which de Chardin speaks about, truly plays a constructive role in our transformation. Note that whereas Jesus hollows himself out freely, we *endure* our hollowing out. But He is with us in this process which makes us like Him.

Most Sundays for Mass I join my sick brethren in our nursing home. Their diminishments are the result of strokes, dementia, accidents. One man, a tower of strength in his day, is blind and crippled: everything has to be done for him. At the Sign of Peace he waves a hand, waiting for someone to grasp it in Christian companionship. In Communion he receives into his broken body the broken body of Christ. His hollowing out is almost complete. To watch such men is to contemplate the Passion: what's going on is deeply mysterious yet strangely strengthening.

THE DYNAMIC OF THE CROSS

Naomi Klein's recent book on climate change is titled *This Changes Everything*. In Christian thinking, the Good News which changes everything is that, against all human expectation, God raises Jesus from the dead and brings him into eternal glory. God does this to give us hope – the hope is that we too will rise from the dead. Jesus made a decision to accept with patience and love what people did to him, and his Father shows his appreciation of that attitude by raising him from the dead. This reveals the Good News that changes everything. In a nutshell, it is this: love is stronger than death, and *unavoidable suffering, lovingly endured, turns out to be life-giving*. This is what Christian tradition later named as 'The Law of the Cross'. By law here is meant, not an imposed system like a traffic law, but an inner dynamic that operates again and again for our good. In other words, we are given a guarantee that is based on what went on in Jesus' passion: that day turned from Bad Friday to Good Friday because Jesus bore his agonies with loving endurance. The Good emerged not at the time but on Easter Sunday morning when the Father raised him from the dead. Since we share the same humanity, our suffering and our dying are also transformed when we endure them with love. *They become life-giving*; they bring life to us, and through us to others. We cannot prove this on a scientific level, but there are deeper levels than science and God is at the bottom of everything, always working to bring good out of bad. Saint Paul is trying to articulate this dynamic of the Cross when he asserts that he is *glad* to suffer for others (Colossians 1:24) – he believes that the love that this demands will be life-giving for the rest of us.

What has this to do with good decision-making? For myself, I find that it is I who must decide how I shall bear my sufferings – my arthritis, my angina, my overall slowing up. My attitudes vary from slow-burning resentment or patient acceptance, even perhaps a smile. It is my choice.

DIMINISHMENT AND DIVINISATION

Diminishment, then, involves a great deal of enduring: it is in the enduring that choice comes in. A friend of mine was suffering from Alzheimer's. One evening I asked him how he was doing. 'Well, I often find myself wanting to be done with it all. I'd love to pick up a cancellation on the next sky train.' This may sound morbid, but in fact he was struggling to accept rather than to resist what was happening to him as life spiralled out of his control. His diminishment, patiently and lovingly accepted, is making room for his divinising. God is at work in my friend's pain. In the depth of his heart he is growing in love, even though it doesn't at all feel that way. He wants God the way a parched tongue wants water.

Patient endurance doesn't feel much like loving, but it is. I spoke of Pedro Arrupe earlier and how he had had a stroke in 1981. He endured relentless diminishment for the final ten years of his life. He wrote:

More than ever I find myself in the hands of God. This is what I have wanted all my life from my youth. But now there is a difference – the initiative is entirely with God. It is indeed a profound spiritual experience to feel myself so totally in God's hands.

This surely is a reflection that emerges from a discerning heart! In his poem 'That Nature is a Heraclitean Fire and of the Comfort of the Resurrection', Hopkins captures the fragility and the glory of the human condition:

I am all at once what Christ is, since he was what I am, and This Jack, joke, poor potsherd, patch, matchwood, immortal diamond, Is immortal diamond.

Diamonds are formed through tremendous pressure exerted on coal, which in turn was formed by similar pressure on the remains of great forests. There is an intrinsic link between diminishment and divinisation. By divinisation I mean the process by which we *become like God*. This becoming like God is the big news in the New Testament. We are to become the children of God (John 1:12); we shall become like God when we see him as he is (1 John 3:2). Nothing less than a divine makeover is in store for us at the end!

 Unavoidable suffering, if patiently endured, is life-giving, but the choice is mine.

EXERCISE: THE BLANK PAGE

This little exercise can help you to take a positive stance towards your diminishments.

I invite you to take a blank sheet. On the top left write, 'Dear God' and at the bottom right put your name, and underneath it 'Amen'. Let the space in the middle be filled – in imagination at least – with the history of your life, its activities and accomplishments, its endurings, its sufferings, and its dyings. Hand all these over to God, and ask God to bring good out of them.

The final word, Amen, is richer than we think. It is a stamp of firm commitment. Here it says, 'Lord, this is the song of my life. It's flat in places and I have bungled the words here and there, but it's me. I love you and dedicate my song to you.' In the legend of St Jerome's meeting with Jesus in the desert, Jesus asks Jerome what he has to give him, and Jerome mentions his labours, his penances, his prayers. Silence ensues, then Jesus says, 'Give me also your sins!' Absolutely everything can be included on my blank page!

Our days and years are like the waterpots at Cana: they need the creating word of God to be turned into 'the best wine'. God can and will do this. So your *Amen* can mean, 'Dear God, I hereby commit my life to you, in all its shades, bright and dark. I trust that in your goodness and compassion you will transform it all into something worthwhile.'

I do this exercise occasionally, and it brings me deep consolation. It is a fundamental choice for God here and now; it expresses my trust in God's unconditional goodness and inexhaustible patience. Better for me to do it when I can, rather than delay until I am incapable of making choices any more.

You can do this exercise on behalf of people you love who cannot do it for themselves, or who died suddenly and unexpectedly. One of my colleagues recently collapsed and died at the age of forty-six. He was at the height of his career, and from what I knew of him, death was far from his mind. Recently I led an ecumenical service for him attended by his numerous friends, but today I will hold a personal service for him on the lines sketched above, offering him and every detail of his life to God.

 Dear God, I commit my life to you, past, present and future, in all its shades, bright and dark. Please transform it into something worthwhile!

HEALTHY IMAGES OF GOD

I notice that deep in my heart I can be wary of God. Is God really dependable? Can I name God as truly Unrestricted Forgiveness? Has God *nothing but good* in mind for me? We need to work through the difficulties we experience in trying to trust God. Unless we do, we will find ourselves rather like an acquaintance of mine who remarked: 'God and I don't get in one another's way. I do my thing and God does his. Of course, I like to touch base with him occasionally, but not about anything serious, you know!' Life remains shallow as long as we keep God at a distance and avoid allowing God any role in our choices. We can create images of God which are no more than human projections: instead we need to let the real God speak. But once again it is a choice.

Bringing God into our decision-making presupposes a healthy image of God: otherwise we can find it too risky! In the introduction I suggested a working image of God: it is, of course, inadequate, as images of God must necessarily be, but not too distorted. I suggested you think of a loving parent, who was always watching out for your best interests, was wise and resourceful, and who helped you unobtrusively to grow into the fullness of your freedom and potential. I added that if you yourself are a parent, this image can be very rich for you.

It is time now to draw together the various indicators scattered across these pages to build up our picture of the real God. But first a challenge to yourself, to explore and spring-clean your operative images of God, because images give rise to beliefs and actions.

What images of God are you *actually* working from? Two examples may help. In her bestselling book, *Eat, Pray, Love*, Liz

Gilbert explains how, when asked what kind of God she believed in, she responded: 'I believe in a magnificent God!' Her story shows that she operated out of that core image in her ways of relating to God. By contrast, G. W. Hughes in his *God of Surprises* suggests that many Christians operate out of an image of Uncle George, a thoroughly unpleasant uncle who demands a Sunday visit under threat of torture.

Do either of these dramatic images help you to identify your own? Or is your god so anaemic and dull that it carries hardly any image at all? When you devoutly or distractedly say 'I believe in God', do you mean that God is a remote being up there, who plays little part in your life, is unmoved by your difficulties, and who certainly doesn't answer most of your petitions? Do you act as if God is small-minded, critical, demanding, preoccupied with sexual matters and with sin? Is your deity unable to cope with the messiness of your life? 'God is alive and well and working on a less ambitious project' – so ran a famous graffito some time ago. Is your god only a pumped up version of a human authority figure? In short, is your operative image of God too small, and would you wish instead to operate out of one that is a bit more magnificent?

LET THE REAL GOD SPEAK!

Since God is totally beyond us, all images are provisional, but God chooses to be self-revealing. The God revealed to us in the Hebrew and Christian scriptures is relational, involved, loving and caring. God's first words to Adam and Eve are, 'Where are you?' (Genesis 3:9). It is important to notice the tone of this question: it is not the confrontational questioning of a law enforcer: rather it is the anguished cry of a distraught parent looking for a lost child. The question expresses a loving relationship on God's part – a desire to find Adam and Eve and to hold them as close as the prodigal father who clasps his wayward son on his homecoming. Again, the Exodus story reveals a God who is concerned about the sorry plight of the

Chosen People and works mightily to rescue them. The God of the prophets cares endlessly for an exiled and wayward people who won't listen. God is the shepherd who cares for all his sheep, especially those who are lost. Jesus, who is the self-portrait of God, is totally relational and does all he can to bring life and hope to everyone: 'he went about doing good' (Acts 10:38). He is the person who loved me and gave himself over to death for me (Galatians 2:20). The New Testament closes with an image of God as victorious over all evil, who wipes away all tears and gathers us into the 'holy city' in eternal joy (Revelation 21 and 22).

Pause for a moment and notice which of these images appeal to you.

In these pages I have tried to be faithful to the God portrayed in revelation and in the best of Christian tradition. My operative theology is that:

- God is the great lover who wants to give us all that we can receive.
- God is busy, active, interested, close, concerned, capable, and engaged with us.
- God is provident and wise, wrestles with evil, and works for our good.
- God has made us for what is good, so when we are moving towards the good we experience joy.
- God deals directly with us – as Ignatius found – to help us make good decisions.
- God wants us to use our freedom well, and accepts whatever decisions we come to. If they are bad, God labours to change our hearts and to bring good out of the damage we may have caused.
- God seeks our collaboration to bring the world to rights.
- God can be found in all things, because God is behind everything that exists.
- God has one single saving project for the human race, and within that plan God works with us individually.

GOD MUSES WITH US

If we can accept all this, we can rely on a God who is active everywhere and who helps us in making our choices. 'What are human beings that you are mindful of them?' asks the psalmist in surprise (Psalm 8:4). While he wonders why God should bother about us and our small concerns, he is very clear that God does so. God is the Lord of history, and the scripture writers interpret the history of the Chosen People in the light of God's involvement. Of course, unlike us, God does not have to race around making billions of decisions to keep the world on course: presumably God, who is free of space and time, makes one all-encompassing decision, and that is enough. What matters is that our decisions resonate with God's. Since God makes us free, God 'waits' on our choices and is pleased when we consult him.

God orchestrates scenarios so that we may get the right insights. We may feel it a restriction that God has a will of his own. Let's be clear that there is a divine agenda – but it is simply for the good of the world and for each of us. God works away at this agenda, undeterred by unhelpful interventions. God could say to me, 'The people you are making decisions for – including yourself – are MY people, so please refer your decisions to Me for approval!' God respects us by listening to us, and invites us in return to listen to divine promptings. God encourages in us a contemplative stance – an openness, the listening ear of a disciple. God yearns to reveal to us what is the wisest and most loving thing to do in any situation, no matter how messy it is. When you muse over a problem, you can well imagine God as musing with you, turning over possibilities, weighing with you the merits of each option, so that finally God and yourself decide together what seems best to do.

 When we mull over a problem, we can well imagine that God is musing with us.

 # 'WHAT ABOUT THE WILL OF GOD?'

THE PROBLEM

Perhaps the last section about healthy images of God seems unreal to you? When we were young we may have been taught that the will of God is rigid, harsh, unfeeling, non-negotiable and implacable. I had an early introduction to this unhealthy image of God when a neighbour lost her eight-year-old child to acute meningitis. My image of God as a celestial Santa Claus was severely challenged. 'If God does this sort of thing to someone only a little older than me, then I am sure in for it,' I thought. 'And if God's mind is made up already, what's the point in labouring to make good decisions?'

And only recently I had a discussion about the Great Hunger; not alone did people die horribly of starvation and disease, but many were treated brutally and denied the help they could have been given. My companion told me that some historians now use the term 'providentialism' to explain it all away – in other words, the whole thing was 'an act of God' so nobody should be held accountable. Every time a disaster occurs, whether the AIDS epidemic or a tsunami, the easy explanation is that this is God's punishment on a sinful world. But who then would want to turn to such a God and look for help to make good choices?

WHO HARDENED HIS HEART?

To interpret rightly the meaning of the will of God is a delicate matter. Let us say a few things about it, to situate our efforts at discernment in a right setting. In the Judaeo-Christian tradition God is understood as free and as having a will. This is the essence of being a person. The writers of the early books of the Old Testament give the impression that whatever happens is God's will. They are trying to preserve the truth that there is no god as mighty as the Hebrew God. This forces them to assert, for instance, that it is their God who hardens the heart of Pharaoh, so that he will not let the Chosen People go (Exodus 4:21; 10:20; 11:10). To think that God causes evil is decidedly primitive theology, but the early writers were doing their best to indicate that Yahweh is unrivalled. Their simple solution was to say 'God does everything!' Likewise, only from a primitive viewpoint could God be thought of as ordering the destruction of the nations whom the Hebrews dispossessed in their effort to gain control of the Promised Land.

A VENGEFUL FATHER?

False images of God are fatal in the world of decision-making. Most importantly we need to read correctly the stance of the Father in the Passion of Jesus. The Father has been portrayed as being angry with the human race: his decision is that if the everlasting punishment we deserve is to be averted, the Son must substitute for humankind by enduring the most savage of deaths. Thus the divine wrath would be appeased. This is a total distortion. In fact Father and Son are totally in love with one another and with the world they have made, so they agree that the Son should become human to save the human race, even at the cost of creating suffering in God.

Jesus does not set out to die for us, but he knows his values will set him on a collision course with those who hold contrary values. As he tells his troubled disciples at the Last Supper, no one shows greater love than the one who lays down his life for his friends, and this is what he will do. In Gethsemane he reacts very humanly against the horror of crucifixion, but affirms the commitment he and his Father had made because they both love the world to the uttermost. Their agape-love will not be deterred by our malice. Instead, the Passion reveals what agape-love is all about. The message is that divine love encompasses human evil, and this gives hope to all of us. Martin

Luther King expresses this truth: 'Hate cannot drive out hate, only love can do that.' There is no angry God checking on us, searching out our weaknesses. There is only Pure Love. God simply wishes us happiness: this is 'the will of God' toward us! The true will of God is Good News for everyone, sinner and samaritan alike.

BUT DOES GOD PUNISH?

With these false images out of the way, we can ask whether God punishes those who do wrong – which of course means all of us. In the less sophisticated images of Genesis God's reaction to human wickedness is portrayed in terms of regret: 'The Lord was sorry that he had made humankind, and it grieved him to his heart ... So he said, "I am sorry that I have made human beings"' (Genesis 5:6-7). God is then imagined as deciding to make a clean and fresh start with Noah after the Flood. This however doesn't work out too well: Noah's descendants don't exactly distinguish themselves in virtuous living. Next, God tries to instruct the Chosen People on how to live rightly, but that doesn't get too far either. God realises, almost with shock, that 'the inclination of the human heart is evil from youth' (Genesis 8:21). The resolution of this dilemma must lie elsewhere!

Hebrew thinking moves on: the Chosen People try to interpret their history in terms of reward and punishment. But this doesn't get too far: the alert ones notice that it is the good who suffer, while the wicked get away – literally – with murder! The suffering and death of the innocent begins to make some sense only when the idea of life after death slowly emerges. Perhaps only then, the Hebrews wonder, the bad will get their comeuppance and the good their reward. This buys some patience and it is allowed that while God certainly delays in executing divine retribution, at least at the End justice will be finally done. Hence the all-too-human notion of a punishing God retained its place – and unfortunately is still alive and well in the old Catechism statement that at the end of time God will reward the good and punish the wicked.

THE DIVINE PROJECT

But there is another twist. We can imagine God reviewing the manner in which the Hebrews portray divine justice, and being quite unhappy about it. We all want to be known as we really are, and so does God. God is *nothing but love and compassion*, and to show this clearly God decides to intervene in person to reverse the cycle of human decline and wickedness and thus bring the human story to a triumphant conclusion. But this will involve reversing all human notions about justice. There will be, in God's intention, no final division of humankind into saved and damned. Instead, God's bright idea is to have the Son 'take away the sins of all the world' (John 1:29). Mercy and love will encompass all wrongdoing. But this was too much for some writers in the early Church, so parts of the New Testament inevitably read simply like an extension of the Old.

Over the centuries preachers have tended to take the hard line – 'You do the crime, you do the time!' – and so the Church has spoken with a very faltering voice about the possibility of the salvation of everyone. It is too much for human thinking. It is easier to get your head around the simple notion that God will punish all those who deserve it. Saint Augustine had a field day on this, and calculated that only a minority would escape divine punishment – which hardly made the Gospels 'Good News' for us sinners.

EVERYONE SAVED?

There is, however, a deeper strand in the New Testament. It says that God has a plan which will be Good News for *all* the human race. 'God wills that all people be saved' (1 Timothy 2:4). Jesus, whose mission is to take away the sins of all the world, promises 'to draw all people' to himself through his death (John 12:32). We can have hope for universal salvation because God is investing everything in this enterprise.

However, Jesus' approach to this task seems not too practical. He goes about doing good, but this angers those who have a stake in the oppressive status quo. Jesus wants everyone to be free from domination so that they can become their best selves, and so he has to stand up for the rights of those who are dominated and diminished. Soon all goes horribly wrong, and after a short public life, Jesus is executed with criminals, buried and wiped off the face of the earth in a well-sealed tomb.

And then comes yet another twist! In his dying, the innocent Jesus accepts his horrible death with patience, dignity and forgiving love. Next comes the extraordinary news that he has returned from death, the same yet different; alive, but in a new and total way. He brings not condemnation but reconciliation.

'YES, YOUR WILL BE DONE!'

All of this brings us to a new understanding of God's will. When we pray the Our Father we ask that 'Thy will be done.' Now we know that what God wills is the salvation of all humankind. This is God's simple and radical intention. Everything else that God wills is to help in achieving that cosmic intention. When we experience goodness of any kind, it is God who is behind it, to help us. When we experience suffering and evil, we are right to believe that God is working to bring good out of them. That is the message of the Passion: Jesus certainly does not want suffering and evil – he cures the sick, expels the demons, liberates the deaf and dumb. But he does not eliminate suffering and evil. Instead God chooses to respect even the bad which we bring to one another, but to bring good from it. How, we often do not fully see. We live in mystery, but it is holy and hope-filled Mystery and based on the historical fact of Jesus' death and Resurrection.

Divine planning is comprehensive – all aspects of reality are included. In each person, no matter how depraved, is a hunger for life, for unrestricted goodness and happiness. Each of us is already God-oriented, and God is always drawing us. God deals with each of us directly, as well as orchestrating human history as a totality.

God can intervene personally in human affairs, as the Incarnation shows. Sin, suffering, evil and death are not outside the scope of divine planning: they are included and woven into it. At the core of human history, that changes everything. Catastrophe yields to joyous resolution, tears and darkness to laughter and light.

Our lesson is that God is to be trusted, and that making our decisions with God rather than making them alone is the right way to proceed. God indeed has a will, and it is firmly set on our good. God is working to achieve the universal happiness of the human race, with resources that are hidden yet powerful and sufficient. God can do everything, because God's dreams stretch infinitely beyond our own (see Ephesians 3:20).

BACK TO OUR CHOICES

We could say, 'Well, that's great. Let's sit back and let God get on with the job!' But this is precisely where we come in. God has no intention of 'doing it all alone'. Paul says that the power of God *is working within us* to achieve the divine purpose. Now we can see that this is what discernment is all about. We are to allow ourselves to be guided by the Holy Spirit, so that in everything we do, including the little things, we edge the divine project towards completion. This is what it means to be disciples of Jesus, to be part of the divine family. We are no longer servants but God's friends.

There are 2.4 billion Christians in the world today. Insofar as they are in tune with God, the divine project of creative good community moves forward.

 God has no intention of 'doing it all alone'. The power of God is working in us so that we can play our role in achieving God's purpose.

CASE STUDY: PITIED AND CHOSEN

Jorge Bergoglio – elected pope in 2013 – joined the Jesuits in 1958, at the age of twenty-two. His exceptional leadership qualities were soon noted, and he was chosen as Provincial of the Argentine Jesuits at the age of just thirty-six. His six-year term of office, 1973–1979, was set against the background of some of the most difficult years in the political history of the Argentine. The hierarchy largely supported the government's approach, in the hope of ridding the country of communism. Jorge worked tirelessly for the unity and development of the Province and won the loyalty of most of his men, but also upset a considerable number. Some Jesuits saw him as reactionary and unwilling to engage in the struggle for structural justice. He acknowledged later that his strong style was divisive and had hurt many, many people. 'I did not always do the necessary consultation. My authoritarian and quick manner of making decisions led me to have serious problems'.

He had known that he was seen as a 'problem person' within the Jesuits and, when in Bavaria for studies in 1986, he was captivated by a painting of Our Lady serenely untying the knots in a long white ribbon. What the knots in his own life were he understood only later. But while there he decided to cut short his studies and return home, believing that this was God's call. This decision did not work out well, and at the age of fifty-four he was suspended from teaching and sent to Cordoba in June 1990, with the humble title of 'spiritual director.'

He was deeply hurt by being removed from Buenos Aires and by the dismantling of the good structures he had laboured to put in place. He became depressed and struggled against desolation, that sense that he was drifting away from God. His work with the helpless poor deepened his own sense of powerlessness. He tried to be patient, to trust in God, to take each day as it came. He fought against the temptation to wallow in victimhood, or to take up arms against his 'enemies'. He realised he must leave all in God's hands. He lived in the atmosphere of the Passion of Jesus, experiencing nothing to encourage the hope that the Resurrection was near at hand. He was a 'suffering servant' as portrayed by Isaiah, and endured a place of great darkness and tribulation, 'where there is no solution other than to hope against all hope', as he said himself.

Cordoba was a place of humiliation which led him to truth and humility. These two years of exile and emptiness gave him ample time to reflect on his previous history. He came to see that his style of proceeding had, in his own words, 'hurt hundreds of people'. He was truly, in his own eyes, a sinner, rather than someone who had been unfairly dealt with. The time in Cordoba was a struggle with desolation, but he emerged from this valley of darkness convinced that God had nothing but mercy for him, had forgiven him everything and was inviting him into close companionship and service.

His world changed in June 1992 when he was made Auxiliary Bishop of Buenos Aires. The Jesuits were astonished: the poor were delighted because they saw Jorge as one of their own. Mercy and compassion had become central for him, because he himself had experienced the limitless mercy and compassion of God. He took as his motto, 'Pitied and Chosen'. He was caught by the Gospel scene where Jesus has pity on Matthew, the despised tax collector, and calls him to follow him. Jorge identified with Matthew.

Over the following twenty years he worked with and for the poor, and then, against all the odds, he was elected Pope in March 2013 and took the name Francis, expressing his commitment to the poor of the world.

MY COMMENTS

➤ Although those concerned with Jorge's career were well-intentioned and trying to interpret what God wanted done, things did not work out. Something other than negotiation had to happen, something more personal. Jorge's two years of suffering transformed him and helped to make him the man who as pope has so enthused the world. He embodies the loving and merciful presence of God.

➤ There are dark times when one must wait, pray and trust. It was critical for Jorge to recognise how his heart was being drawn in directions that seemed humanly justified but which, in fact, would have led him away from his true centre – God. It invites me to ask myself, 'What do I do with my hurts and resentments? Am I being led by the good Spirit when I live out of them?'

➤ The poor can be our best teachers. They have nothing human to hope for, and yet they try to keep going. Their areas of effective freedom are narrow, and perhaps for that very reason they often have a sense of God which eludes the rest of us. They are free to let God be close to them.

➤ Pope Francis is a person of unusual inner freedom. This is helping to change our perceptions about the Church, about the world, about ourselves, about how to go about things, about what truly matters. He speaks from personal experience when he says that we are infinitely loved. He affirms the dignity of all, the poor whom he champions and the rich whom he challenges. Because he trusts in God and in people, the strategy of collegiality as a way of decision-making has become the dynamism of his papacy.

YOUR COMMENTS

_____

_____

_____

_____

_____

_____

_____

_____

_____

 What do I decide to do with my hurts and resentments?

 # 'HOW FREE AM I?'

We have already looked at the importance of inner freedom in making good choices. But does God limit our freedom to keep us under control? Consider the following situation, recounted in R. and B. Zander, *The Art of Possibility* (Penguin, 2000).

At the University of Southern California a leadership course was set up for the fifty best students from a total of twenty-seven thousand. No matter how well students performed, the rule stated that only one third of the fifty could get an 'A'. This arrangement appalled Ben Zander, a teacher of music at the New England Conservatory. He had thirty students each year, all of excellent potential, but what he noticed was that many tended to be inhibited instead of creative when they performed. They were fearful, keeping an eye on him and their desired 'A' rather than on their inner muse. In varying degrees they were suffering psychological and emotional paralysis. To liberate them, Zander began his course one year by announcing: 'You will all get an "A" next June!' All they had to do was to write him a letter, imagining that June had already arrived: in their letter they had to explain why they had got an 'A'. This focused them positively towards the challenges of being creative and yielding to the magic of music over the nine months they were beginning.

LIBERATED?

Does this story hint at how it is with us? The liturgy proclaims: 'By your Cross and Resurrection you have set us free.' Is freedom an essential part of the package of agape-love? Is the freedom Jesus has won for us *conditional* or *definitive*? Have we all already been awarded an 'A' – a guarantee of our place in eternal life, so that we do not have to worry about failing the final test at judgement time? Are we liberated from fear and energised to go out and creatively face the challenge to build a better world in the here and now?

Again, what does St Paul mean by 'the liberty of the children of God' (Romans 8:21)? If the freedom that follows from the work of Christ is merely conditional, it's nothing to marvel at. Do we imagine ourselves as being only on parole? Why do many Christians sit around as if still in chains, as if the 'release of captives' (Luke 4:18) had not already taken place? Was it not this experience of liberation that made the Early Christians so happy, and have we lost the sense of it? Acceptance of liberation seems to be difficult for us. But St Paul and the other New Testament writers have a crystal clear message of freedom for us: 'For freedom Christ has set us free' (Galatians 5:1). 'Brothers and sisters, you have been called to freedom' (Galatians 5:13). 'Where the spirit of the Lord is, there is freedom' (2 Corinthians 3:17). Christ's work was 'to free those who all their lives were held in slavery by the fear of death' (Hebrews 2:15). 'Freed from fear and saved from the hands of our foes we are to serve God in holiness and justice' (Luke 1:71). 'We are freed from the law of sin and death, (Romans 8:2). 'If God has acquitted us, who shall condemn us?' (see Romans 8:34).

NEW IDENTITY

'The wind/Spirit blows where it chooses, and you hear the sound of it, but you do not know where it comes from or where it goes. So it is with all who are born of the Spirit' (John 3:8). Those born of the Spirit are to be as free as the wind. Saint Paul uses the term *parrhesia* (meaning 'freedom to say everything' and 'bold confidence') to illustrate the point. The Spirit is given to each of us, making us fully adopted children, expelling the spirit of slavery (Romans 8:14-17). This means that as a child of the house I can dash around, in and out of my father's study, whereas the slave child cannot. Because of the work of Jesus I am given the confidence to act as a son or daughter of God. Jesus had that bold confidence – he could look his Father in the eye, know that the Father was totally on his side and that he could depend on him even in the worst of situations. *Jesus knew that he was free*, and since we are now family, sons and daughters of God, 'we are to walk just as he walked' (1 John 2:6), and trust in the freedom that is given to us.

So we have a new identity. We are a chosen race. (see 1 Peter 2:9). But chosen races are free, so we *are* free. Jesus' goal is a domination-free world; this includes our liberation from all that can oppress us, including our fear of being denied entry into eternal life. This requires an abandoning of the warped image of God as the stern judge who waits to punish and condemn us if we sin. Christian life is a fresh start. Religion is no longer seen as primarily our striving but as a joyous responding to what God is doing for us. Divine energy is freed up in us to become a gift for the world.

'BE FREE AS I AM FREE'

Jesus used his freedom to serve the human race. We are to use our new God-given freedom likewise. We are freed to be fully at service, not simply 'to do our own thing'. Freedom is not for licence but for love. The meaning of discipleship is made clear: according to von Balthasar, one of the great recent theologians, the command, 'be perfect' means 'be free as I am free.' It is as if God were saying, 'I am free, and I use my freedom to bring joy to humankind. Go and do the same.' Freedom is a gift that carries a profound responsibility. We are to exercise our freedom in partnership with God.

There are, of course, limits to freedom. We mentioned earlier the distinction between essential freedom, the prerogative of every person, and *effective* freedom, which is affected by circumstance. We noted earlier the limitations that both Sheila and Cathy experience as they make their awkward way along. Effective freedom may be reduced almost to zero, yet essential freedom remains. Jesus highlights this for us, and that is a great help. Nailed to the Cross, his only freedom was interior: he had to wrestle with himself to plead for forgiveness for his torturers. He could have hardened his heart and he could have cursed his God. Instead he held firm: he forgave his torturers and entrusted himself to his Father. We have mentioned Nelson Mandela, imprisoned during the apartheid regime in South Africa. He describes this time as his 'twenty-seven years holiday' and retained his inner freedom, even to the point of rejecting an unworthy release after twenty years.

The precepts given to the people of God are very few. God's mercy has willed that we should be free. These are the words of St Thomas Aquinas and are used by Pope Francis in *The Joy of the Gospels* (n. 43). We are to live out unburdened lives in the presence of God. Like the music students mentioned, our creativity can then come to full flower, the possibilities of which we did not dare to dream can be taken up, and live our lives to the full, rather than simply acting out of a small portion of ourselves.

 Suppose you felt truly free: how creative could you then be?

'WHO'S IN CONTROL HERE?'

Life can be bewildering; we rarely know what's coming next, and many things don't turn out the way we anticipate. John Henry Newman affirms serenely that 'God knows what he's about'. But often God's ways make little sense to us. Living by faith doesn't give us a smooth passage, even though it offers us a new way of seeing things, and a new way of approaching our difficulties. So questions arise: Are human affairs dependent on chance? Can God be responsible for *everything*? Is discernment a vain effort to keep our balance in a chaotic world which is in fact outside our control? Does God play dice with the world? What about the notion of unpredictability introduced by quantum physics? And what does it mean to say, 'Whatever will be, will be?' or 'If it's in the plan it will happen!' Does God's plan roll on independently of our choices? Who is in control of my life, God or myself?

A woman told me the following:

Our marriage was dead after twenty-five years. Rigor mortis had in fact set in long before that, but I couldn't admit it. Since then I thought long and hard about terminating it officially, but after arguing the plusses and minuses with myself for a year or more, I stayed with my partner. Why? Well, I am a Christian, and I know we are told by Jesus to love one another. We simply failed at that – clash of temperaments, I suppose – but we had three children, two boys and then a girl. The boys are living abroad, and I couldn't bear the idea of my daughter being landed with my partner if I walked out – he's a chronic invalid, and she hasn't married. I love my daughter, and after all, it was my marriage, not hers. I also felt that it would be right for me to stay with him rather than to leave him. Could that be pure love – I mean 'pure' in the sense of having hardly any emotional resonances?

Was this woman free in her choice? Was God waiting for her to make the 'right' decision or was he watching and supporting her over the years? If she had changed her mind at some stage, would God have wavered in loving regard for her?

Can we say that instead God is the great strategist who sets up our world so that we can choose well, while also respecting our freedom? Look back to Ignatius for a moment: how did it happen that there were no romantic novels for him to read when he was convalescing? Was this pure chance, or did God play a part in it? How did it happen that there were in fact two good books there, *The Life of Christ* and *The Lives of the Saints*, which caught his imagination and set his soul 'ablaze with God' as he puts it? Does God provide good possibilities for us, and then wait to see if we pick them up? If we do, God is delighted; if we don't, does God try another route until we catch on?

Ignatius spoke of himself as being an obstacle to God's work. He says this: 'Nobody can calculate the degree to which they impede and undo the effectiveness of the Lord's influence on themselves.' He is referring to 'delicate thoughts and insubstantial things ... which seem slight and almost completely unimportant, being so faint' (*Writings*, 161–2). Contrary and negative influences can impede and undo the subtle play of God on our hearts. This reflection of Ignatius leaves me with the feeling that perhaps I am often like a third-rate musician who plays along without attending either to the score or the conductor!

GOD'S GAME PLAN

God factors human freedom into the scheme of things. God prompts us toward good decisions, but whether we choose to attend or not is our choice. God's core prompt is that in every choice we should be in tune with love – not with *any* sort of love, but with self-donating agape-love. To be in tune with love is to be in tune with God's project, and that project is a society in which everyone is valued, respected, included, enabled to reach their full potential and to be happy.

God is not upset by probability or chaos theory: for God, the universe is open-ended, full of creative possibilities. God could exploit these possibilities alone, but chooses instead to enable us to do so with him. God invites Adam and Eve to take over and to increase, multiply and fill the earth. This is an amazing invitation that could destroy the harmony of things, and does! But God favours subsidiarity and is not hierarchical or controlling. As previously stated, God's project is more like a football manager's game plan than an architect's blueprint. De Chardin chose the term 'directed chance', which leaves room for our spontaneity and free will, for probability and chaos theory, while preserving an over-arching order. God does not roll dice! For more on this see Joseph Bracken SJ, *Does God Roll Dice?: Divine Providence for a World in the Making*. (Liturgical Press, 2012).

We are to be co-creators with God of an unfinished universe. Since God already envelops our universe there is no need for us to seek to be transported elsewhere to find God. God is the divine milieu, the environment for created reality. But this level of inter-relationship means that we affect others by our decisions and actions, and are affected by theirs. The future is what we shape by our choices. At the end we will see for the first time just how important our decisions have been. The universe and the Kingdom of God will have their eventual shape because of our decisions. In his book, *Lonergan and the Level of Our Time* (University of Toronto Press, 2010) theologian F. E. Crowe uses a strong image to indicate the importance of our decisions.

My every action has its eternal aspect. Every idle word and every passing thought become part of the granite mountains of the universe of being; they do not vanish into the past but remain and are in eternity. With every moment we are building eternal reality, adding another brick to our house of being. In daily converse we try to forgive and forget, but the universe of being cannot forget ...

'Every idle word and every passing thought ...'. This should stop us in our tracks occasionally. Earlier we quoted Hopkins. He was surely referring to the ups and downs of his own life in the description, 'This Jack (*of all trades*), joke (*people laughed at him*), poor potsherd (*broken clay pot*), patch (*an old word for a fool; also a bit of cloth*), matchwood (*it crumbles under pressure*). What a description of a failed life! Yet it is an 'immortal diamond' because of the motivation of love behind it all. Love carries into eternity (1 Corinthians 13:8), and shapes the final arrangement of things. No matter how chaotic or disastrous our lives might be, 'our good deeds go with us' (see Revelation 14:13), and then, like the water in the pots at Cana, they are transformed by the touch of God.

CAN GOD CONTROL EVIL?

How does God cope with evil and the misuse of human freedom? This is a huge topic, but let us repeat that God chooses not to eliminate evil but to transform it from within. God is a transforming God. The tsunamis of evil, sin and death are encompassed by the greater ocean of divine love. As we said in speaking of the dynamic of the Cross, the Friday on which Jesus was crucified is named 'good' *only* because the loving attitude of the victim brought limitless good – the salvation of humankind – out of the evil of his death. God 'controls' evil by squeezing the poison out of it, or by taking the sting out of it, as St Paul puts it (see 1 Corinthians 15:55).

God controls evil because God has a single plan which accommodates everything, including the aberrations of human freedom. We can't imagine what God's mind must be like, given the problems we fail to cope with ourselves. Try getting a small family organised to go on a holiday, or try to find a plumber at the weekend! But God is simply God. Karen Armstrong opens her book on *The Case for God* (Knopf, 2009) by quoting the reproach of readers who had waded through her previous books. 'That book was really hard!' they said. 'Of course it was' she wants to retort: 'it was about God!' I quoted Liz Gilbert earlier, who said, 'I believe in a magnificent God!' Magnificence can be hard for our limited human minds to take in.

 With every choice we are building eternal reality.

CASE STUDY: THE MAKING OF A POPE

As the Conclave neared which would elect him pope on 13 March 2013, Jorge Bergoglio was aware of the remote possibility that he might be chosen, despite his age. He knew this because at the previous Conclave in 2005, the number of votes he had received was preventing the then Cardinal Joseph Ratzinger from reaching the required two-thirds majority. Some discernments have to be made in a very short time-frame, and on that occasion Jorge's freedom from any desire for power had enabled him to ask his supporters to give their votes to Ratzinger, lest an election stalemate should bring disunity to the Church.

Now, in 2013, he kept a low profile in the pre-Conclave discussions, except for a short intervention in which he outlined the options for the Church. It could, he said, become self-referential and thus lock Jesus in; alternatively it could look outward and bring the Gospel to a needy world. As the balloting proceeded, it became clear that Bergoglio would be the chosen man. To the cardinals he appeared to be calm and tranquil. Later he said, 'Although I'm the kind who worries, who gets anxious, I was at peace. This confirmed to me that this was the will of God.' He accepted his election, saying, 'I accept, even though I am a great sinner.' The theme of being flawed yet called had reappeared. As he made his way towards the balcony and the waiting crowds, however, he found himself 'seized by a great anxiety'. He stopped to pray for a full twenty minutes until the storm passed, and found himself flooded with joy and peace. 'I was filled with a great light,' he later recalled. 'It lasted a moment, but to me it seemed very long.'

He added: 'I had a great sense of inner peace and freedom, which has never left me.'

MY COMMENTS

> We can sometimes notice a recurring pattern in our lives, which can be a great support when we doubt how we should proceed. This pattern is set up by God. It remains steady, as if our life – despite all twists and turns – was held together by a golden thread of grace. We do well to try to catch on to it. This intimate engagement of God with our lives is a source of strength, comfort and the conviction that God and I are travelling together on life's journey. Grace comes tailor-made!

> Ignatius, who experienced this consistency in the drawing of God, remarks that God can so move and attract the human will 'that without doubting or being able to doubt, the faithful soul follows what is shown'. Once he reflected on what was going on, he knew that 'the finger of God' was there.

> The joy that Francis experienced on his election, and which radiates from him despite all his challenges, surely comes from God. Saint Ignatius had remarked that 'only God can give consolation to the soul without preceding cause. For it is the Creator's prerogative to enter the soul and leave her, and to arouse movements that draw her entirely into love of his Divine Majesty.' Since no one in their right mind would want to be pope, the source of Francis' consolation was not in the job itself – I that sense it had no preceding cause. It came to Francis as an awareness of 'being with God' which would make the trials of the job bearable. The reassuring promise 'Do not be afraid!' recurs sixty-seven times in scripture, and the promise 'I am with you!' nineteen times. We are not alone.

YOUR COMMENTS

_____

_____

_____

_____

_____

_____

_____

 Have you experienced difficult events which 'put a stop to your gallop' but then opened up a new path for you?

✳ WITNESSES TO THE DISCERNING LIFE

I. IGNATIUS OF LOYOLA

Perhaps because there are few people around to educate us in God's delicate ways, we tend not to notice God's action on our hearts. But Ignatius of Loyola, who became a master in discernment, learned it, albeit slowly. His account of how God communicated with him can illuminate how God is working through us. Then decisions are more easily made which are in harmony with God's designs for the world.

Ignatius' early life gave little hint of what he would turn out to be, and how vastly he would influence others. He was born in 1491 in Loyola, which lies in the Basque region of northern Spain. It was a time of extraordinary development in human consciousness: the Renaissance was under way in Europe, and the New World was being discovered by Columbus, Cortez and Magellan. He was the thirteenth child in a modest noble family. He had to leave home to make a career, went into the service of the local Viceroy, and at the age of thirty was injured at Pamplona and came home on a stretcher. He had intended to distinguish himself in the service of the king of Spain and to woo a noble lady. Now his leg and his dreams were shattered. He was confined to his couch for the better part of a year, convalescing after brutal knee surgery.

He describes what went on during this forced inactivity. We may presume that he could not sleep very well. But during those endless days and nights things occurred that transformed his life. He had little to read, because none of the romantic novels he loved were available. So as we noted earlier, he read the only two books that were to hand, *The Life of Christ* and *The Lives of the Saints*. He became engrossed in them, because they spoke to his chivalrous heart. But he also took time to daydream about the noble lady by whose beauty he had been smitten. Out of this situation there emerged his insights into the complexity of discernment.

ABLAZE WITH GOD

Ignatius describes himself as a slow learner. God was his teacher and had to be patient with him, 'perhaps because of his lack of education and of brains, or because he had no one to teach him'. Ignatius refers to himself in the third person. So it was only after several months that he became aware of contrary feelings in his heart, depending on which of the two topics was occupying his mind – the service of Christ or of his lady love. The notion of serving Christ brought him a joy that remained with him. The fantasy of serving his lady love also brought joy, but it did not last. What he calls his 'first reflection on the things of God' is this insight into the differing moods of his heart, and their sources. Gradually he came to believe that, *through the joy that remained with him*, God was touching his heart and drawing him into divine service. This is how he came to recognise consolation and desolation and stumbled on 'the discernment of spirits'.

It is worth reading his own account in his *Reminiscences*. It can help us to get in touch with our own inner experiences. I am using a translation that faithfully reflects the unpolished text of Ignatius himself, that of Joseph A. Munitiz and Philip Endean: *St Ignatius of Loyola: Personal Writings* (Penguin, 2004).

His Lady Love

In that house [Loyola] none of those books which he normally read could be found, and so they gave him a life of Christ and a book of the lives of the saints in Spanish.

Reading through these often, he became attached to what he found there. On ceasing to read them, he would stop to think: sometimes about the things he had read, at other times about the things of the world he had been accustomed to think about before. And, out of many things which had previously presented themselves to him, one held his heart in such deep possession that he was subsequently absorbed in thought about it for two and three and four hours without noticing it, imagining what he was to do in the service of a certain lady: the means he would take so as to be able to reach the country where she was, the witty love poems, the words he would say to her, the deeds of arms that he would do in her service. He was so carried away by all this that he had no consideration of how impossible it was to be able to attain it. For the lady was not of the ordinary nobility, nor a countess nor a duchess: rather her state was higher than any of these.

Our Lord and the Saints

Still, Our Lord was helping him, causing other thoughts, which were born of the things he was reading, to follow these. For, while reading the lives of Our Lord and the saints, he would stop to think, reasoning with himself: 'How would it be if I did this which St Francis did, and this which St Dominic did?'

These thoughts too used to last a good space, and, after other things between, the thoughts of the world mentioned above would follow, and on these too he would stop for a long while. And this succession of different kinds of thoughts lasted a considerable time.

The Opposing Spirits

Still, there was this difference: that when he was thinking about that worldly stuff he would take much delight, but when he left it aside after getting tired, he would find himself **dry and discontented.**

But when about going to Jerusalem barefoot, and about not eating except herbs, not only used he to be consoled while in such thoughts, but he would **remain content and happy** even after having left them aside.

But he wasn't investigating this, nor stopping to ponder this difference, until one time when his eyes were opened a little, and he began to marvel at this difference and kind and to reflect on it, picking up from experience that from some thoughts he **would be left sad** and **from others happy**, and little by little coming to know the **difference in kind of spirits** that were stirring: the one from the devil, and the other from God.

This was the first reflection he made on the things of God; and later, when he produced the *Exercises*, it was from here that he began to get clarity regarding the matter of the difference in kind of spirits.

Reminiscences, 6–8

Ignatius spent the rest of his life gaining more and more fluency in this language of the heart. Through it he became able to help others notice how God was speaking to them. As Superior General of the Jesuit Order, he spent his days discerning how God might best be served in all sorts of situations. He divided those days into three parts: listening to others; reflecting on what he had heard, and, most importantly, consulting with God on what to do.

You can learn to notice the different aftertastes of your experiences. This is Lesson One in the language of the heart, and God is your Teacher.

MY COMMENTS

➢ *Imagination is important.* Ignatius spent his days fantasising. His lively imagination enabled him to enter deeply into the life of Jesus. He lived out the Gospel scenes vividly. We can do the same, and find ourselves falling in love with Jesus and identifying with him. Then life is changed.

➢ *It is good to stop and think*. It requires discipline, but it's worth the effort. Otherwise our lives are a ragbag of experiences of which we can miss the deeper meaning.

➢ *Suffering is a classroom*. The experience of suffering can help us grow. Ignatius' injury forced him to a painful halt. Sickness, suffering, traumatic events and disorienting dilemmas can do likewise for us. In times of forced inactivity, God gets space to work in us.

➢ *Desires lead us*. God plays on the desires of Ignatius, making one attractive and the other distasteful. If he had had no desires, nothing would have happened. We can reflect on our desires to see which of them leads us towards greater life, towards outward-bound love.

➢ *God is in the ordinary*. In our seemingly ordinary inner experiences and feelings God is drawing our hearts by whispering to us, 'Go this way rather than that!' It took Ignatius a long time to come to the realisation that God is waiting to be found not only in special situations, but everywhere and in all choices. Only at the end of his life does he say that he can find God in *all* things. He was 'always growing in devotion, i.e., in facility in finding God, and now more than ever in his whole life. And every time and hour he wanted to find God, he found him' (*Reminiscences*, 99). Our own growth in finding God is to be progressive also.

➢ *God meets us directly*. God can deal directly with the human heart; in Ignatius' lucid account we see this happening. His little book, *Spiritual Exercises*, stands or falls on the truth of his assertion that the Creator can deal directly with the creature, and also, perhaps surprisingly, that the creature can deal directly with the Creator and Lord.

➢ *No decisions without asking God's advice*. From this single experience of noticing the play of contrary influences on his heart, the world of discernment opened up for Ignatius during his convalescence. He came to see that for him it was not to be an occasional event, but a fundamental way of proceeding. Later he would say, 'We should make no decisions, however small, without asking counsel of God, as from a wise and loving father.' His life became one long discernment as he allowed himself to be 'led by Another', and made his choices in light of what he felt God wished him to do.

➤ *To do or not to do?* While Ignatius used to ask himself, 'What ought I to do about this or that?' he did not have a saviour-complex that drove him to answer every need. Rather, he would talk with God about an issue, and must often have decided that God was not asking him to engage in the matter at all. The point was that if he were needed, he would be available.

YOUR COMMENTS

_____

_____

_____

_____

_____

_____

A SPIRITUALITY OF DECISION-MAKING

Ignatian spirituality, so popular nowadays, grows from this spiritual experience of Ignatius on his sickbed. There he began to notice what was going on in his heart, and later learned to apply God's lessons to the art of making good decisions. In his writings he has left us a rich legacy on our topic. The goal of his little masterpiece, *Spiritual Exercises*, is 'the seeking and finding of the will of God in the disposition of our life' (*Exercises*, 1). He judged it worthwhile, as we have said, to ask persons of generous hearts to spend thirty days in these exercises in order to become free to make good choices. His *Examen* – also known as the *Review of Consciousness*, or *Consciousness Examen* – is a handy, workaday aid in living a discerning life, which helps you to ponder the events of the day, and notice where God was present and how you responded. Ignatian Prayer and the Examen are centrally focused on graced decision-making, and you will find them helpful.

The probing questions, 'What have I done, what am I doing, what shall I do for Christ?' (*Exercises*, 53) express Ignatius' early efforts at discernment. The very asking of them got him going, and constituted the dynamic of his conversion. Throughout his life he dialogued with God whom he sought in all things, especially in his decision-making. His *Spiritual Diary* reveals how he used to chat out his choices with the Holy Trinity. His seven thousand letters are concrete records of his efforts to be in tune with God on a bewildering array of topics, and the *Constitutions of the Society of Jesus* (the Jesuits) were largely written while he was at prayer.

You could usefully read his *Reminiscences* as one person's progression in the art of personal discernment. Notice how his motivation slowly becomes purified and less self-centred as he moves along. So, as we have seen, out of loyalty to his earthly lord he decides that he will defend Pamplona; out of respect for Our Lady he ponders whether or not to kill a Moor who had doubted her perpetual virginity; he decides to imitate the austerities of the saints in order to do penance for his sins; then, won over by the graciousness of God, he decides to offer himself for total service to Christ his Lord. At the end – a year before his death – he acknowledges that he could find God at every time and hour. If you like to have a goal to achieve, this one will do!

ON THE CAMINO

A Jesuit colleague of mine, Brendan McManus, took up the insights of Ignatius in a striking way, as recounted in his book: *Redemption Road* (Orpen Press, 2014) His elder brother, to whom he had been close, had taken his own life. Over several years Brendan mourned for him in quiet desolation. Then there came to him the idea 'I'll walk the Camino, and I'll carry his football shirt to Compostela and leave it there.' This ignited a fire in him and gave him hope that the pilgrimage, with its long days of solitude, endurance and prayer would help him to integrate his brother's death into his own life. He travelled alone, but took Ignatius as a companion all the way. He tried to interpret his daily experiences and to find God in them, and to make his decisions while keeping God before his eyes. Slowly his spirit was liberated from the bondage of grief and guilt. He found God in other pilgrims, in his own inadequacies, in the beauty of things, in the interplay of consolation and desolation. Occasionally he noticed that his heart was being addressed, as when he was about to buy some attractive items in a Bilbao hiking shop. A calm came over him which seemed to whisper, 'You don't actually need this stuff, this merchandise'. Have you perhaps ever sensed that you were being communicated with in regard to your choices? Brendan described the experience as being like putting on new glasses. He saw that he could live very simply and yet be happy.

For the record, he completed his journey, burnt the football shirt, and found peace.

 In times of forced inactivity, God gets space to work in us.

II. JESUS

Jesus of Nazareth was a free person. He was in fact, a person of extraordinary freedom and independence. He was untouched by self-concern – he tells us not to worry because *he himself did not worry* (Luke 12:22-35). This gave him immense courage and unparalleled authority.

We do not know how Jesus came to shape his life as he did. We can only say that from early on he had a unique awareness of God, as we see in the Finding in the Temple, where he makes a radical choice to be about his Father's affairs (see Luke 2:41-52). He enjoyed an incomparable sensitivity to what God would prefer, and seemed to take for granted that life was about responding to the divine call.

Jesus kept God always before his eyes. He had what Solomon had prayed for – a discerning heart. Throughout his life he allowed himself to be led by the Spirit. Each decision he made was an effort to express his love for his Father. So he reveals to us how a discerning heart works. Whatever he decides to do is the fruit of his loving intention to please his Father. Each person he meets is of unique importance to him, because he sees them all as they really are. He makes decisions all the time: to linger in the Temple as a child; to be submissive in Nazareth; to leave home though it breaks his mother's heart; to preach, to work, to pray, to heal, to touch, to feast, to choose certain people and not others as his closest disciples ...

GOD'S POINT OF VIEW

He is so in touch with his Father that he finds him in the most ordinary situations. This is what goes on in the discerning heart – it discovers the divine in the concrete here and now. So in Mark 10:35-45 we find James and John putting Jesus on the spot. They want first places in God's kingdom: but Jesus turns this naïve ambition on its head. He promises that they will experience a high level of closeness to him – but of course this turns out differently to what they expect. He then decides to channel the anger of the other apostles away from a confrontation with James and John, towards a radically new vision of what the reign of God is about. He picks up their desire to be 'great' but recasts it in terms of service to everyone. This, he tells them, is what his own life is all about. In doing this he uses a minor squabble to reveal the Christian ideal of limitless service, which is the divine strategy for the reshaping of the mess that is human history.

Like us, Jesus did not have a divine blueprint to help him in making his choices. In each situation he had to work out what was the wisest and most loving choice. If we had been there to question him about this, perhaps he might have said, 'Well, taking everything into consideration ...' 'Everything' – there is the touchstone of true discernment, as we have said in stressing that there are no purely private decisions.

Thus he had to decide whether or not to gather disciples, and whether or not to risk sending them out in his name, given their limited grasp of his vision. He had to judge whether to make himself endlessly available to others, or to take precious time out to nourish his own heart in prayer. He had to assess whether or not to take on the oppressive authorities of the Temple and the State. Would it be better to play safe and avoid disturbing the status quo of Jewish society? Should he risk his life on behalf of those excluded from the community of his day? And so forth, endlessly.

'WHAT PLEASES HIM'

Jesus operated within a hostile context, but he always did what he felt his Father wanted done, even at the cost of his life. Transparently allied as he was with the Spirit, the divine agenda found its perfect spokesperson in him.

'I always do what pleases him' (John 8:29) is a perfect statement of what discernment is about, and it lays down a marker for us as disciples. Let us explore this expression. First, note its interpersonal quality: Jesus does not say, 'I always do what is right'. What he does is the result of pure love, not out of compulsion or self-glorification. He draws back the veil so we see the intense love that vibrates between himself and his Father. They are totally in love with one another. They chat everything out: the Son watches and imitates the Father. For us too the habit of discerning will give an interpersonal shape to our living. We are in a You-and-I relationship. I am not abandoned to myself – nor should I ignore God and fly solo. Jesus says, 'I can do nothing of myself'! (John 5:30). Am I happy to say that?

'I *always* do what pleases my Father' – this is breathtaking! Jesus is presented as the exemplar of the human person before God, totally open. He wasn't interested in pleasing himself: pleasing his Father was the single goal of his life. The saints tried to live in this dimension, and so can I. Of course I won't always get things right, but even to *want* to please God in everything is already to please God. I can come to walk habitually with God. In the life to come I will be transparently open to God – I will be the instrument, the song of God, like Mary who is described as 'the reed of God'. We can start the process today.

DEEDS OVER WORDS

'I always do what pleases him.' For Jesus, pleasing God was found in doing, not just in thinking or romanticising. 'Love ought to find its expression in deeds more than in words,' Ignatius says succinctly. This openness to *doing* will express itself in pleasing others – not in a sleazy or obsequious way, but in truly *being for them*. I want to please others rather than simply pleasing myself. Why? Because God is always trying to please me. This is what the Incarnation is about – God setting out to please the human race.

Doing the will of God is grinding and demanding only if 'doing my own thing' is the motivation of my life. Doing another's will runs counter to the human desire to be free, unless we act out of love. For Jesus, doing what God wants means yielding to the pull of love at his deepest centre. The discerning person who seeks God's will is like a friend searching the face of the person they love to see what the other would want. Life, for Jesus, is a love affair: the Father is trying to please him and he is trying to please God. 'I do exactly as the Father tells me' (John 14:31) is not the statement of a perfectionist who gets everything right. It is an effort by Jesus to show that his heart is intimately aligned with his Father's. Our task is to approximate that!

In Daniel Quinn's award-winning novel *Ishmael* (Bantam, 1992) the narrator sees an ad in a local paper: 'Teacher seeks pupil. Must have an earnest desire to save the world. Apply in person.' He responds, and the book takes off from there. The parallel to the Gospel invitation, 'Follow me!' is uncanny. The Teacher is present, looking for pupils. Am I up for the challenge of saving the world?

 We should make no decision, however small, without asking counsel from God as from a wise and loving father.

St Ignatius

III. YOURSELF!

It may surprise you to find yourself included in the exalted company of Ignatius and Jesus. But since you are reading this book you are a person already intent on what is good. You do not live just for yourself at the expense of others. No doubt you have selfish tendencies, but you try not to let them dominate. You are trying to serve God, and deeper than that, you are in love with God and you have some sense that God is in love with you. You want to do what is pleasing to God, even if you have your occasional lapses. You have a discerning heart.

As a parent, a worker, a senior citizen, you may not think of your life as particularly significant. Yet yours is a graced life story. There is more to you than meets the eye. You have good desires. You find yourself admiring people who go out of themselves, often alone, to serve their needy neighbour – the founders of movements like the Samaritans or AA, or women and men dedicated to the care of the needy. You admire those who see a human need and do something about it, and those prophets who make a lonely stand for justice. We have mentioned Óscar Romero, but there are so many others. Dorothy Day implored God during a Hunger March in Washington in 1932 to show her how to help build a better society. The next day she met a man with whom she collaborated for a lifetime serving the poor and unemployed. With him she founded houses of hospitality and farm communes. She acted as a gadfly to the conscience of the US Administration, prayed and fasted for world peace, and died among the poor in 1980.

Reading this book, you will have allowed your heart to be touched and challenged. Perhaps you have been moved by the simple but profound ideal that nudged Ignatius 'to help others'. What will you do with the years you have before you? Certainly your family, your career, your happiness, your economic security have to be carefully considered. Yet you may wish to do as the early Christians were invited to do, 'to put your gifts at the service of others' (1 Peter 4:10). Perhaps you feel that you can make only a small difference, but that will be enough. By serving God's people in any way, you will please God, as Jesus did.

BECOMING LIKE JESUS

The same Spirit of God that led Jesus to 'go about doing good' (Acts 10:38) wishes to lead you to do likewise. God is always trying to break in on your consciousness. If you have *the mind and heart of Jesus* (Philippians 2:5) you stand for God's values, which are centered on loving compassion. You are to love and forgive, serve others in their needs, build an inclusive and sharing community, and stand for the rights of the oppressed. This requires that you use your freedom responsibly, read the signs of the times, cultivate honesty of heart, love God in prayer and deed, and let your light shine in the world.

With guidelines such as these, Jesus charted his own life. You can keep your eyes on him, as a good disciple would, and take your cue from him. If you say, 'I want to help others', yours is already a heart that is open to discernment.

You may feel powerless to influence other people; there is comfort in knowing that Jesus often felt likewise. But he always tried to bring *life* to those he encountered (John 10:10), and you can too. He knew that 'for God, nothing is impossible' (Matthew 19:26), so he never despaired of people. He laid himself on the line and trusted his Father to convert human hearts to love. He interceded for his enemies, and he still intercedes for the world. You can pray to be 'led by the spirit of God' as he was (Romans 8:14).

THE MYSTERY OF YOUR TRUE SELF

To be 'led by the Spirit of God' is to be led into mystery. But I hope that by now you are convinced deep down that God has nothing but good intentions towards you, and will 'not lead you into temptation, but deliver you from evil' (see Matthew 6:13). God's intention for you is simple but wonderful – that you gradually become your true self! You are an extraordinary immortal, as C.S. Lewis puts it, 'a mystery of religion'! God is hidden in you now, but in God's good time you will be 'revealed in all your glory' (see Romans 8:18). God's project is to bring everyone into everlasting joy. The word 'mystery' carries profound weight for St Paul. He speaks of the mystery hidden from all previous generations, but revealed to the first Christians. This mystery or secret turns out to be God's loving intention to save everyone. It is a plan 'for the fullness of time, to gather up all things in Christ, things in heaven and things on earth' (Ephesians 1:10). 'Gathering up' does not mean that God will round us up like scattered sheep! Instead it hints at our transformation, our becoming like God. We are already the images of God, but *incognito*. Then we shall be fully revealed as the daughters and sons of God.

THE MEETING OF TWO WILLS

Discernment has a deep quality of mystery about it, because it brings God awesomely close. It involves the interplay of two wills: one will is divine, the other – your own – is very human. So discernment spans two worlds, the human and the divine. God's world embraces all reality, past, present and future, and God is infinitely wise, imaginative, enabling and caring. By contrast your world is tiny, bounded by space and time, and you can be less than wise and imaginative, and your care can be limited to those you know and meet with locally.

Christian discernment, then, is not an exercise between *equal* partners. Instead you, a small creature, are tapping at the door of the Creator for help with a choice you want to make well. The door opens; you enter; you speak and are heard. And then you listen. It's like learning a song, the melody of which haunts you with its beauty. It is as if the three divine Persons are singing, and you are trying to catch on. You come away hoping that you can remember the harmony and sing it in your place and time.

What Jesus seems to have had from early on in life, we only slowly get hold of. He was always in harmony. The divine and the human intersected perfectly in him. The love that moved him to his choices came from above. Consulting with his Father was the norm for him, while for us to allow the divine to intersect with our own desires takes time and labour. Much self-emptying has to go on in you, even to want it. You may feel it's unrealistic to try to live consciously in harmony with God. It puts you out of step with your culture. It can help to read Henry David Thoreau's *Walden*, who in 1846, at the age of thirty, took two years out from public life, and lived at Walden Pond, a small lake in Massachusetts, where he engaged in an inner voyage of self-discovery. He later wrote: 'If a man does not keep pace with his companions, perhaps it is because he hears a different drummer. Let him step to the music which he hears, however measured and far away.'

You have your very own music that plays within you. Most of us are afraid to step out and dance to our own beat. If you are depressed, tired, or unhappy, is it because no one has helped you to attend to the 'far away music'? It is always there, and when you listen to it and dare to move with it, life opens up. You can now interpret, even if only awkwardly, the language of the heart – your passion, your desires, your dreams and hopes. You are waking up to God and to the play of great love within you. You are in touch with the music that is soundless. God helps you by providing companions who also sing the song you are hearing. You may seem to make little impact on a world full of violence and tragedy. But since it seems to please God to work silently, you are in tune with God, and that is what matters, what changes the world. Listen to this wisdom from the contemplative tradition:

What each one is interiorly, face to face with God, unknown to anyone, is of vital consequence to all.

And every act of love, every act of faith and adoration, every mute uplifting of the heart, raises the whole world nearer to God.

From everyone who is in union with God, there breathes a spiritual vitality, light, strength and joy, which reach from end to end of the universe; a source of grace to those least conscious of it, even to those least worthy of it, and knowing nothing of how and whence it comes.

This reflection is about you! You are part of the web of humankind stretched across the globe. You have an interior life, you speak with God about the things that touch your heart, and you can rightly believe that all of this brings life to others. You are a living member of the communion of saints, and just as divine energy has come to you through others, energy flows through you to many others in return.

 Discernment spans two worlds: the human and the divine.

SUMMARY OF THE DYNAMICS OF PERSONAL DECISION-MAKING

Our choices are to be at once *both loving and wise*. This is how God makes choices about the world, as in the Incarnation, but also as regards ourselves. God has a single project that embraces everything. Divine discernment is always **creative** ('Let it be'); **loving** ('God so loved the world as to send his Son'); and **life-enhancing** ('I come so that you may have life to the full'). Our decisions are meant to share these qualities.

The dynamics involved in making good choices are as follows:

- ➢ I need the **desire to serve God** and to discover what God may wish me to do in a particular situation.
- ➢ I need a reasonable level of **self-awareness**. I ask God to help me to be in touch with my desires, both the good and the wayward ones. I ask for light to distinguish between my own concerns and the concerns of God or of others.
- ➢ I need **clarity about the option** and **the relevant facts**, while allowing that the future is veiled from me in many ways.
- ➢ I need **inner freedom**, to be able to take up either option. If I am not free, discernment goes no further.
- ➢ **I match the options against the Gospels** to see which fits better. Which choice would better bring 'Good News' to those affected?
- ➢ I set out **the arguments *for*, then the arguments *against*** the option;

> **I give time to prayer**, asking God to show me what is best to do. How much time? As much as I can manage!
> I try to notice the contrary pulls of **consolation and desolation**. What is the aftertaste of my pondering either side of the option? On which side do I find **energy, joy, peace and love**?
> **I wait for God** to give me clarity, rather than push the issue.
> **I test the proposed decision** over time, through consultation with others, and noticing the movements of my heart. 'Can I, at my best, live with this?'
> **I implement the decision**, while being open to revise it if the situation alters significantly. God's will is more important than my own decisions.

Here I offer some general reflections on the cases scattered through the preceding pages. Recall the girl who would become a butterfly; Sheila and Cathy who had communication issues; the woman who used to say 'This is no concern of mine'; Barbara and her negative feelings; Óscar Romero, the unlikely radical; the quiet Trappists faced with death; the respectable who lack soul; King Solomon and the baby; Ann who wanted to work with the dying; Jorge Bergoglio who learned humility the hard way and later accepted election as Pope Francis; the music students who needed an 'A'; the woman whose marriage had died; Ignatius who was torn between God and his lady love; Jesus who always tried to please his Father; myself as I wavered about going to Somalia and later got an insight about perfectionism; and yourself as you try to respond to God's music.

> Something was stirring in each heart. It was God hoping to be heard. Each person was helped insofar as they caught on to the language God uses, that of consolation and desolation. The light always 'shines in the darkness' of our searching or troubled minds. The experience of inner unhappiness is not to be rejected out of hand, because it has a dynamic quality, nudging us to get our life into better order. Inner turmoil is at least a sign of life.

> The challenge to achieve authenticity is ongoing: God doesn't let up on us but calls us to move beyond our self-imposed limits and boundaries. God, who is creative love, is drawing each person to an outward-bound love, which is life-enhancing. Which of our characters paid attention and gave the time needed for reflection? Which of them was prepared to risk changing a settled, if uncomfortable, way of life? Which of them was free enough to choose their best option?

> The issue of healthy relationships is a common thread in all these different cases. It so happens that what makes God happy is good relationships. The three divine Persons enjoy the best of relationships among Themselves and they want us to be happy too by building good relationships with one another and with Themselves. When you find decision-making tough, ask yourself a single question: 'Will this option or that bring about better relationships?'

YOUR INSIGHTS

I suggest that now you take a little time to write down here the ideas or phrases that have touched your heart. Imagine you have a briefcase that you are filling up with documents for your journey of discipleship as you follow Jesus along the Christian Camino! Jesus said to his disciples after the miracle of the loaves and fishes, 'Gather up the fragments, so that nothing may be lost!' (John 6:12), so please do this now.

 Listen to the gentle and quiet whisper of God that comes after the hurricane, the earthquake and the fire.
See 1 Kings 19:11-12

And so we bring our exploration of **personal decision-making** to a close, and move into the area of **group decision-making**.

PART TWO

GROUP DECISION-MAKING

✳ SEARCHING TOGETHER FOR GOD

I. BUT WHY GET INVOLVED?

Part One dealt with the dynamics of *personal decision-making*. Now we will move on to apply these dynamics to *group decision-making*. It has been suggested that some eighty-five million meetings occur daily across the globe. Whatever about that figure, innumerable decisions are made daily, and they shape our lives and the future of our world to a greater or lesser degree. Think of UN debates about imposing severe sanctions on a member nation, or a government planning a hair-shirt budget, or an international conference divided on the issue of global warming. Participants may have their own private ethical convictions, but they will be under pressure from various quarters to vote by expediency rather than principle. What can we say of such meetings? Who will be speaking in support of God's agenda, which may involve the good of everyone on the planet and the planet itself? What do you make of Dag Hammarskjöld's statement: 'In our age, the road to holiness necessarily passes through the world of action'? And how do you react when you hear comments such as the following:

> ➢ 'Faith should be kept out of politics.'
> ➢ 'Look at the damage religion does when it gets dragged into public affairs.'
> ➢ 'We learn enough religion to hate, but not enough to love, so let's leave it out!'

> ➤ 'One lone voice will never be heard!'
> ➤ 'You won't find God at meetings. God's busy only in churches and holy places!'
> ➤ 'In our times, corporate holiness is needed to serve the Kingdom of God!'

If you are someone who already engages in public issues when required, you need not spend long on this section. If, however, you need encouragement before stepping outside your private world, I offer the following myth:

An Iroquois myth tells of a moment in the tribe's history when the council of the braves met to decide on where to move for the next hunting season. The place chosen was in fact occupied by wolves, which attacked and killed many of them. The remaining members had to choose: either kill the wolves or move elsewhere. The first choice they rejected, because it would make them the sort of people they did not want to be. And so they moved on.

To avoid repetition of their earlier error, they decided that in all future council meetings someone should be appointed to represent the wolf. The contribution of the representative would be invited with the question, 'Who speaks for wolf?'

How does this story impact on you? Might it be your task to 'speak for wolf' – to be a voice for some person or group that would otherwise remain unheard? 'Wolf' can stand for the excluded, and every society has its own share of them – people who are marginalised, unwanted, ignored. Their number is legion. 'Wolf' can also stand for God. Could it be your task to represent God at a meeting? This would be both an exciting and demanding challenge. When Jesus sent his disciples out on their mission, he was depending on them to make his Good News known across the nations. They were 'to speak for wolf' – in this case, himself. Of course he would be with them but they were to be his voice.

If you accept the challenge to speak for God, and learn the necessary skills, you will find that meetings are transformed. You will have a new lens with which to view what is going on, and you can at least help to focus the group towards what is most desirable. Behind this you will have the sense of partnering the Good Spirit in the daunting task of shaping a better world.

'WHY ME?'

It comes as a surprise to most Christians to be told that they are meant to be actively engaged in the concerns of the world. Yet that is the teaching of Vatican II, and that Council is already half a century old. To be saved, you don't have to be a Christian, but if you are such, you accept that God needs your help in transforming the world. Human affairs are God's affairs too: that is why God gets personally involved with us in becoming human. As stated in the Vatican II document, *The Church in the Modern World*:

> *The joys and hopes, the grief and anguish of the people of our time, especially of those who are poor or afflicted, are the joys and hopes, the grief and anguish of the followers of Christ as well. Nothing that is genuinely human fails to find an echo in their hearts.* (n. 1)

Prior to Vatican II, rank-and-file Catholics were consigned to passivity. The slogan was 'Pray up, pay up and shut up!' But the Church is coming of age, and now we are asked to be proactive and to witness to God's dream for the human race. The Holy Spirit supports us as we try to discern how best to do this. The Spirit attends all meetings, not only 'Churchy' ones, and can speak through anyone of goodwill. But the Spirit expects Christians to be especially available to undertake the task of transforming a broken and pain-filled world. In the authentic Christian tradition, passivity, lethargy and hopelessness are not an option, because God engages in the divine plan to bring the world to rights.

ARTISANS OF A NEW HUMANITY

A few quotations must suffice to indicate the challenge that Vatican II puts to every Christian.

> *With the help of divine grace, there will arise **a generation of new men and women, the artisans of a new humanity** – The Church in the Modern World, 30.*

> *Lay persons are to be **heralds of a new heaven and earth** – Church, 35.*

> *Each individual layperson must stand before the world **as a witness to the resurrection** and as a sign that God lives – Church, 38.*

> *The laity should **collaborate** with all men and women of good will – Laity, 8.*

> *Everywhere the laity must **bear witness to Christ** and give an answer to everyone who asks a reason for their hope of eternal life – Church, 10.*

> *All disciples of Christ are obliged to **spread the faith** to the best of their ability – Church, 17, Missionary Activity, 23.*

'LET NO ONE REMAIN IDLE!'

Twenty-five years after the Council, St John Paul II, aware of the resistance within the clergy to sharing their power with their people, wrote *The Vocation and Mission of the Lay Faithful*. Its guiding image is the Gospel parable of the vineyard, with its leading question: 'Why do you stand here idle?' The response is 'because no one has hired us', to which the owner of the vineyard replies: 'Go you too into my vineyard.' No one, says the pope, should remain idle in face of the needs of our times. Each person is uniquely called by the Lord to do now what Christ did in his time: to promote the kingdom of God, and to participate in the work of creation. The People of God are to be *co-workers* with God for the good of the world. Aware of their own unique dignity, *the laity are to promote the dignity of the human person everywhere* (36, 37).

'WHAT TO SAY?'

Of course, if you do go into the vineyard, you need to know how to manage the vines. So where can you learn what best to do in regard to even one of the issues that arise? The Gospels require us to care for the poor, to stand for the dignity of every human being. But how best to do this today? Happily, there is a wealth of Christian social teaching that could help to transform political, economic and social life: but it seems to be a well-kept secret! The deeper your grounding in it, the more wisdom you will be able to bring to issues. And if you're not the 'expert type' you can still access knowledge at short notice, if you know where to look. If in doubt, phone a friend!

II. WHAT CAN ONE PERSON DO?

Personal witness is worth much more than a deluge of words. To show that one person can make a difference let us take one among innumerable examples.

Kevin Boyle, 1943–2010, was born in Northern Ireland. He lived much of his life in the shadow of the Troubles which ravaged the community and left three thousand dead. Atrocities and violence reigned. He decided to become a specialist in law and criminology but he developed too a keen sense for the democratic means to achieve peace. For him this involved more than theory: he put his life on the line, and marched for civil rights in 1969. He was attacked and abused for his troubles. He tried to coordinate a movement for civil disobedience, then went to study and lecture in the US, where he saw police racism and discrimination of black communities close at hand. The streets of Detroit reminded him of the ghettos of Belfast, so he returned to Ireland in 1974, and set up the Irish Centre for the Study of Human Rights, advised on the New Ireland Forum which tried to promote dialogue between the opposing sides, and worked with Amnesty International. He travelled to South Africa to report on the apartheid regime. One of the pioneering legal minds in Ireland and the UK, he took cases to the European Court on killings by the security forces. A tireless advocate for human rights, he was named Human Rights Lawyer of the Year in 1998, and was advisor to Mary Robinson in her role as UN High Commissioner for Human Rights. His work has had a far-ranging effect on many people and continues to bear fruit.

He had an inner instinct for making good decisions and for persuading doubting or hostile colleagues of the best way to go. He came to meetings well prepared, stuck by what he believed to be the right path to take, and won people over by his conviction, vision and dedication. While he worked passionately for the rights of others he respected his adversaries and gained their grudging respect in return.

Take a moment to see if you can identify someone you admire, who has played a role in what we have termed 'social decision-making' – that is, someone who stood, perhaps alone, for the values of truth, justice, inclusion, peace. Kevin Boyle 'spoke for wolf' – may we do likewise!

POPE FRANCIS

Pope Francis catches up the tradition of the Second Vatican Council and of St John Paul II, on the role of the People of God in the contemporary world. While Vatican II and St John Paul II urged the 'laity' to play their part in 'secular affairs', Pope Francis goes much further in his manifesto for the Church, *The Joy of the Gospel* (2013). There he challenges all the People of God to become evangelisers.

Each Christian and every community must obey God's call to go forth from our own comfort zone in order to reach all the 'peripheries' in need of the light of the Gospel. (n. 20)

[A parish must not become] a useless structure, out of touch with people, or a self-absorbed cluster made up of a chosen few. (n. 28)

Where is your brother or sister who is enslaved? Let us not look the other way. There is greater complicity than we think. The issue involves everyone. (n. 211)

STOP TO THINK!

Notice what goes on in your heart as you read the above. Do you find in yourself a desire to 'speak for wolf'?

We spoke earlier about consolation. Saint Ignatius compares consolation to a drop of water falling on a sponge, and desolation to a drop of water falling on a stone. What do you notice as you reflect? Perhaps you find yourself wondering, 'Francis is saying I'm important to the world! I don't know what to do, but God will show me.' Do you feel all right about this? Does it give you a sense that this is what your life is meant to be about? If so, you are experiencing consolation.

You may instead notice that you are a bit upset. This is what Ignatius means by 'water splashing on a stone'. Do you find yourself muttering, 'I can't do this. It would shake up my whole way of living. I know I have talents and can express myself well, but quite honestly, people with causes turn me off. I'll make a donation to charity instead, and then I'll feel better'? But perhaps you don't feel better after doing so! You may feel ill at ease about being in God's presence, as if there was a clash between what God wishes you to do and your own desire.

If you take a static view of your role in the Church you will piously ignore the pleas of Councils and popes to play your part in the emerging world. If God is remote and uninvolved, you could legitimately sit back and let the world go by. But God says, 'I know what's going on: I don't like it, and I am going to get something done about it!' So he calls Moses and tells him to bring the Chosen People out of Egypt. Moses tries to decline the invitation politely, and says, 'Who am I to do this?' To which God replies, 'Just go and do it. I will be with you!' (Exodus 3:7-12). We are dealing with that self-same God as Moses encountered three thousand five hundred years ago.

I sometimes wonder just in what way God communicated with Moses. On the first occasion the voice spoke from the burning bush, and this got Moses' attention. Subsequently was the communication less dramatic? Did he experience something compelling in his mind and heart? However it was, we have today the help of conscience, inner sensitivity and the guidelines given by Jesus and interpreted by Ignatius to enable us to interpret the present time (Luke 12:56) and make life-giving decisions. Freedom is God's greatest gift to us. We are to use it for the common good. God will respect our best efforts and will work with us. A student at a course on decision-making wrote up a comment which I treasure, as it illustrates both the pain and the deep joy that can come when we get involved.

> I used to hate meetings, so I avoided them when I could. When I did attend, I was always noticing the negatives: the Chair's poor preparation or performance; individuals pushing their private agendas; others waffling or giving off toxic messages. I hated the tension and I hated bad decisions. But something changed in me recently when I began to think of finding God in all things. This wasn't just saying that if you look hard you'll find God hidden in nice things. It was more that when you make your best decision you make God to be present and active in a situation. There's something fresh about all this for me – that God is engaged everywhere, shaping the world through us. I'd never thought about this: God was a kindly but distant figure for me. Now I think of God as an enabling God, and I'm his hands and feet. Also that since meetings matter to God, they should matter to me, no matter how I feel about them!
>
> I still find them hard, but they're not dull any more. I go because I believe God is struggling there and I should help him. I try to get the best possible outcome, so that people, especially the vulnerable, are really helped. I have developed some skills and I try to keep my eye on God. That helps. I'm naturally quiet and thoughtful, not great on my feet, so I try to think things out before getting there. I pray a bit too. It's a shock

to believe I'm helping to build a better world at a meeting, and that I'm not on my own. God is backing me up. Wow!

 God is involved in human affairs, and expects me to be available for service.

III. IS GOD PRESENT?

Can we believe that at every meeting, *bidden or unbidden, God is present*? The Swiss psychoanalyst Carl Jung, who borrowed the saying from the sixteenth-century Catholic writer Erasmus, was so caught by this assertion that he hung it as a plaque above his front door. Could it be hung at the entrance to the UN, the White House, the House of Commons, the Stock Exchange, your own boardroom? We tend to doubt this. God seems absent from the world of politics and international economics.

And yet it's true that God is present in every meeting place, bidden or unbidden. Why can we be sure? Because the world and all its people belong to God who makes and sustains them. And God does not leave us to our own devices: the scriptures tell the story of God's involvement with what God calls 'my people', and that involvement will never end. The Incarnation is the dramatic sign of Jesus walking 'among his own' (John 1:11), and when he affirms that he is 'with us always' he means it. Where two or three are gathered in his name, he is present (see Matthew 18:20).

BRIGHT WINGS

But how is Jesus present? It is through his Spirit, who works with our spirit, the divine dimension of us. At a meeting each participant can attend to the voice of conscience, which is the whisper of God, and can thus distinguish right from wrong. The Holy Spirit is everywhere at work, even if incognito or ignored. In 'God's Grandeur' Hopkins puts it well: 'The Holy Ghost o'er the bent world broods with warm breast and with ah! bright wings.' This 'brooding' is an image of the Spirit's closeness to us: it is like that of a nesting bird, and enables our best desires to hatch and to take flight. As Christians we can bring the mind and heart of Jesus not only to our individual decisions, but to whatever meetings we attend. When we are tuned into the 'frequency' of the Spirit we can introduce people of goodwill to the same frequency.

We previously spoke about the need for prophetic voices. God is always looking out for persons who will speak up on behalf of divine concerns. Over and over in Hebrew history God calls people to act as prophets. 'Get up,' says God to Jonah, 'and go at once to Nineveh, and cry out against it' (Jonah 3:1). We are all called to the task of prophecy: that is, not to predict the future, but to be voices for the well-being of humankind. We may not like this task, but that is another matter, as we shall see shortly. If all Christians were prophetic, that would make 2.4 billion witnesses to Gospel values in a world population of 7.3 billion! To be prophetic is to share something of the imagination of God. We find in scripture that God has surprising ideas about how human being should interact: the goods of the world are to be shared; hatred is out and forgiveness is in; equality is to replace domination; rulers are to serve; and irrespective of merit or failing, all are invited into the final banquet. When small groups of Christians grapple with the imagination of God, surprising results can emerge.

TERMS

Within the vast scope of group decision-making we can draw a distinction. We will use the term **social decision-making** to cover a situation *where an individual – like yourself – is trying to speak for God by using the dynamics of Christian discernment within a secular framework.* Think of an anti-drugs group, a multinational corporation, a political party, a non-denominational school, a boardroom, a family dispute about money. The challenge is to believe that a lone voice can enable divine concerns to be heard in such a setting; that one person, speaking out of a conviction born of faith, may help a group of people to make a good choice.

We will then turn to **communal decision-making**. By 'communal' we mean that a group of *believers, faced with a common challenge, are* *trying to find their way forward by discernment.* Think of Vatican II, the longest and largest meeting ever held, where some two thousand five hundred bishops and their aides worked for three years to hammer out the *aggiornamento* of the Catholic Church. Think of the trustees of a Catholic fee-paying school who are considering entering the free education system, or of a parish pastoral council debating how to respond to the development of an Islamic community within the parish boundaries. Think of religious orders, dioceses, schools, parishes, the Society of St Vincent de Paul, Christian advocacy groups. Each group gathers periodically to see its way forward with God's help in the light of changing realities. God is 'coming at us' in everything; God lives in open system reality, and God is full of bright ideas. In praying and sharing on the Gospels we begin to allow God to take centre stage in our planning.

What sincere groups have in common is that, at least implicitly, *they want to do what God would wish.* Since God thinks globally and also cares about each individual, they try to also, as best they can. The members are open – in varying degrees – to divine values, even if no formal process of discernment is being followed.

 When you share the imagination of God you enter a new and exciting world.

DECISION-MAKING IN THE CHURCH

I. TOWARDS COMMUNAL DISCERNMENT

When I was younger I had a certain innocence in regard to the Church. I thought that its decision-makers would want to do only what God wanted. One of the great shocks of my life in the years since Vatican II was to find that the concerns of the real God – as revealed in scripture and especially in the life of Jesus – are sometimes ignored by those in power when making important decisions.

If you want an exciting read, take up *Vicars of Christ: The Dark Side of the Papacy* (Corgi, 1990) by Peter de Rosa. If you choose, dismiss it as 'a bin full of garbage' as one critic did. But then try Luigi Accattoli's *When A Pope Asks Forgiveness* (Paulist, 1998), and learn how St John Paul II apologised some ninety-four times for the sins of the Church! These sins include:

> ➤ the Church's support for the Crusades, for the Inquisitions, for corrupt dictatorships;
> ➤ the Church's persecution of Jews, Muslims, Latin-American Indians, Galileo, the Reformers, and non-believers;
> ➤ the role of the Western Church in the Eastern Schism; religious wars and the fomenting of divisions among the Christian Churches;
> ➤ the Church's attitudes to women, to slaves, to black people and to the world's poor.

This shameful litany would be significantly added to in the following decade with the Church's apology for clerical sexual abuse and its cover-up by those in authority, all done 'for the good of the Church and the avoidance of scandal of the faithful'.

The list on the previous page is not an exhaustive list of the Church's sins. The faithful everywhere have endured the misuse of religious power; this clericalism is described by Pope Francis as the cancer of the Church. Our beloved Church stands *always in need of reform*, as Vatican II points out in the *Decree on Ecumenism*, (n. 6). We publicly profess that we are set on God, and not any God of our own construction, but the God of the Judaeo-Christian revelation might not recognise our attitudes and actions as owing much to Christian revelation. We cannot be naïve about the difficulties in making good decisions, and about the challenge to pride, power and small-mindedness that is involved. The shock of realising how dismally we fall short of what God wants of us can galvanise us into tackling the dark shadows and becoming truly 'the light of the world'.

NOT AN INCH

There can be a tendency for some members of the Church to be very resistant to change, but not John Henry Cardinal Newman who, writing as far back at the nineteenth century, declared that: 'Ideas ... continually enlarge into fuller development ... In a higher world it is otherwise, but here below to live is to change, and to be perfect is to have changed often.' Elsewhere he remarks that 'growth is the only evidence of life'. We humans are learning beings, never fully arrived. We need to use our freedom and intelligence to inch towards the fullness of truth, which turns out to be a Person, God! Vatican II is a landmark illustration of the fact that the Church can and must grow in her understanding of the Mystery she carries and of her role in the world. J. R. Noonan's book, *A Church that Can and Cannot Change* (Notre Dame, 2005) is an enlightening read. He takes up such issues as slavery, religious freedom, marriage and usury, and shows how the Church has changed its teaching on them over the centuries. All law, he says, must be open to change, in order to serve love better; love is the one moral teaching that cannot change.

Since God delights in doing new things (Isaiah 48:6) I must be open to new things too, as Jesus was. When God looks around for help in bringing about a 'new thing' does my hand shoot up to say, 'I'm here, send me!'? This was young Isaiah's response when he was overtaken by the majesty of God in the temple (Isaiah 6:8). Is it mine, or must God look elsewhere?

'WHAT'S THIS ABOUT DISCERNMENT?'

Pope Francis is in tune with Newman. He wants the People of God to engage together in the task of making the Good News known to the world. But since the Good News *will always* be new, the embedding of it in different times and places will bring us into uncharted territory. Since new issues will come up for decision as history unfolds, the pope's proposal is that *these decisions should be reached by way of communal discernment*. The word 'discernment' occurs more than twenty times in his Apostolic Exhortation, *The Joy of the Gospel*.

Never before has the theme of discernment been so highlighted by a papacy. Perhaps this is not surprising, since Francis is the first Jesuit pope, and so he is a follower of Ignatius, a man who, as we have seen, practised the art of making good decisions. So discernment is now dramatically brought to the centre of Christian life in our time. If an old Church is visibly dying, the new Church which is slowly emerging will, if Francis has his way, be 'led by Another', which is what discernment is all about. For Francis, Christian discernment is the only way forward for the Church. Discernment puts the *divine agenda* before any human agenda. We are to be led by God in all that we do, and we are to discern together as a single people of God. This gives us a new understanding of who we are – not passive recipients of Church teaching, but creators of it!

The pope does not set out the theory of discernment – he seems to assume that his readers will understand what he means. It is part of his Jesuit mindset, and he wants it to be ours. But in fact his call to discernment marks a seismic shift in the government of the Church, or rather a return to its foundations. In the Council of Jerusalem, about AD 50, representatives of the early Church seemed to take it for granted that they should work together with the help of the Holy Spirit through a particular and far-reaching disagreement. However, this practice of communal discernment was soon lost; authority-figures made the decisions and so the People of God were silenced. The Ecumenical Councils, however, show discernment at work, if only in a limited degree.

Vatican II was a highpoint in communal discernment, even though not explicitly so. The participants were not asked formally to take time out in order to notice the movements of their hearts around the innumerable options they faced, nor was the importance of their inner freedom underlined. John O'Malley's classic book *What Happened at Vatican II* (Harvard University Press, 2008) does not include the term 'discernment' in the index. Neither does the term appear in the indices of three recent biographies of Pope Francis. Truly, the emphasis on ecclesial communal discernment is new, and will have a difficult birth. It will help if we understand it well so we can play our part in it.

OPEN TO THE SPIRIT

Pope Francis was elected in 2013 through communal discernment. The conclave that chose him, an unlikely candidate given his age, was certainly open to the Spirit. In his turn he not only stresses the importance of communal discernment but witnesses to it in his collegial style. We can explore its parameters by listening to what he says about it in *The Joy of the Gospel*:

➢ The totality of the faithful have an instinct of faith – *sensus fidei* – which helps them to *discern* what is truly of God (n. 119).

➢ Every Christian and every community must discern the path that the Lord points out (n. 20). Local issues of discipline are to be *discerned* by the relevant bishops, rather than by Rome (n. 16).

➢ Wise and realistic *communal pastoral discernment* should be undertaken, especially under the leadership of the bishop (n. 33).

➢ Each Church is to undertake a *resolute process of discernment* to make the missionary impulse ever more focused, genuine and faithful (n. 30).

➢ In *discernment* we find the path of the Spirit and understanding of the Gospel (n. 45).

➢ We can choose between a clinical and neutral process of evangelising, or an evangelical *discernment*, nourished by the Holy Spirit (n. 50).

➢ *Discernment* will entail allowing oneself to be guided by the Holy Spirit, renouncing the attempt to plan and control everything to the last detail, and instead letting him [the Spirit] enlighten, guide and direct us, leading us wherever he wills (n. 288).

A CHALLENGING AGENDA

Discernment in common is challenging to us all:

➢ It is an acknowledgement that it is *God* who leads the Church, not the pope or the hierarchy, nor some faction within the People of God. As a Church we must all allow ourselves to be guided by the Holy Spirit, who 'leads us into all truth'. The Holy Spirit joins with us in our discerning. We must not attempt to plan and control everything to the last detail, but let the God of surprises lead us to what is best.

➢ Discernment is an exercise of the power given to the Christian community as Christ's body. The People of God have a right instinct in regard to matters of faith. This instinct is both gift and responsibility. Conversion of heart and good listening are required to achieve the level of openness that discernment demands.

➢ Every group is to discern at its own level, following the principle of subsidiarity. A local group discernment must be respected by

higher authority. Not to take it appropriately into account would be to impede the dynamic of the Spirit's work within the Body of Christ.
➤ The task of evangelising is difficult, but common discernment generates energy, mutual support and a shared joy in the knowledge that what is being done is what God wants done. When all the members can say, 'With my whole heart I seek you: do not let me stray!' (Psalm 119:10) the sense of unity is very evident.

Wherever there are Christians, the practice of discernment should be alive and flourishing. Francis' images of the Church are earthly – the field hospital, the mother, the tired and muddy traveller, and so forth. It is in the ebb and flow of earthly life that God is to be found. While God seems to delight in disguises, hiddenness and silence, Francis is pointing up some of the surprising places in which God may be found by those who discern together.

CREATING AN ATMOSPHERE

Personal discernment is a prerequisite for communal discernment, otherwise the latter is paper thin. With his Ignatian background and his personal struggles, Francis is well poised to make the best use of communal discernment. Such discernment is adaptable – it may be formal or informal – and since he came into office he has been labouring to create an atmosphere of communal discernment within the Church. He is doing this in many different ways:
➤ *Collegiality:* Francis has embraced the call to collegiality, which ran aground soon after its approval in Vatican II. One of his first actions was to create an advisory group of eight cardinals to share in the administration of the Church.
➤ *Open Discussion:* His synodal style is an effort to counter the monarchical image that has characterised the Church for the past millennium. He is engaging all the People of God in the task of finding the way forward together. The Extraordinary Synod on the

Family in 2014 contained many aspects of communal discernment: the global consultation of the faithful; the prayerful setting; the encouragement of honest sharing of views, even if conflicting. Good listening was encouraged; straw voting gave hints of where the wind of the Spirit might be blowing; openness and clarity were promoted through making the proceedings available to the participants as an aid to preparation for the 2015 Synod.

➤ *Global Communication:* Francis' appointment of new cardinals from the furthest reaches of the world indicates his wish to have all voices in the Church heard. The question, 'Who speaks for wolf?' is answered from the ends of the earth, rather than from Europe alone. Those on the periphery will now be heard. Further, cardinals are to be servants, not princes: they are to listen to and work with their people, not lord it over them.

➤ *Inclusion of the Poor:* Francis believes that the Church must be anchored in the 'ordinary faithful' and the poor. The poor are close to God: they have a sense for God and so have much to teach the Church. He wants the people on the margins to find the Vatican accountable to them, and not the other way around.

➤ *Evangelisers All!:* Francis is a pastoral leader – he is not trying to do everything himself, nor does he 'go it alone'. He is engaging all the faithful to share the divine command to spread the Good News to all the world.

➤ *A Listening Church:* It is clear that for Francis, God must lead. We must listen and search for what the Spirit may be saying to the Churches. For him this involves both personal prayer and listening to others, including those who dissent from our own preferences. Only thus, he believes, will hearts be opened to divine promptings.

 God wants community to flourish in the Church and the world. Communal discernment can bring this about.

II. ENTER THE LAITY

As we have seen, for Pope Francis the laity are meant to be major players in the task of discernment. This involves the retrieval of a great truth that has been long obscured. A recent Church document, *The Sensus Fidei in the Life of the Church* (2014) prepared by the International Theological Commission and approved by the Roman curia, explores the implications of this truth. It is quite an explosive document.

The Latin phrase *sensus fidei* means 'the sense of the faith' or 'the appreciation of the faith'. In popular terms it says that the whole body of the Church has 'a nose' for the truth. Together, the People of God, laity and hierarchy have an instinct which enables them to zero in on the essentials of faith. It enables them to recognise and endorse authentic Christian doctrine and practice, and to reject what is false. Not everyone may be able to give arguments for what they hold, nor refute contrary arguments, but they 'know' in a heartfelt way what God wants them to hold. This is a knowledge born from love for God and from their living Christian experience.

Vatican II makes it clear that there is one universal call to holiness, and that the Holy Spirit enlightens every member of the Church. *Together* the members can make the decisions that foster that holiness. The early Church was aware of this truth, but it became buried over the centuries as the hierarchy assumed the task of teaching and the laity were reduced to the status of passive learners. We are now regaining the belief that the People of God, – whether taken together, in groups, or individually – are the temple of the Spirit (Romans 8:16). The Church doesn't depend on hierarchy, much less patriarchy, to be true to itself, because everyone has the Spirit dwelling in them. Within this basic equality leadership becomes *servant leadership*; all leadership is in the service of love, and the ultimate Leader is the Spirit.

NEW WAYS

In his first Angelus address, Pope Francis quoted the words of a humble, elderly woman he had once met. She had said, 'If the Lord did not forgive everything, the world would not exist'. His admiring comment was, 'That is the wisdom which the Holy Spirit gives'. The woman's insight is a striking manifestation of the instinct of faith. Moreover, the faithful have a sense for what Pope Francis has called 'new ways' for the journey of faith. Bishops and priests need to be close to their people on the journey so that they may recognise these 'new ways' as they are sensed by the people. The discernment of these will be vital for the new evangelisation.

NOT MAJORITY OPINION

This faith-consciousness is not born out of majority opinions. The 'faithful' are those who are trying to live out their faith. They are at the heart of the Church, they listen to the Word of God, they pray, they listen to the teaching authority of the Church. They are seeking to build up the Church, and to be open to the prompting of the Spirit. They are humble rather than dismissive of views other than their own. They live by joy rather than anger as they seek the truth. Confusion about the right way forward, especially around neuralgic issues such as women's ordination, must lead to further investigation rather than a slamming of doors by either side. In the meantime, interim solutions may be tested out, to see from experience which way God may be beckoning.

A LIVING CHURCH

All the above gives a rich sense of what a discerning Church might look like, whether local or universal. When the voice of the laity is heard and truly respected, the sleeping giant which is the People of God will come alive. The following elements will be present, even when there is principled disagreement about the issue at hand:

> Energy to grapple intelligently with difficult issues;
> Humility, openness, willingness to listen; common searching;
> Appropriate engagement of all concerned, each being respected for what they can bring to the table;
> Sympathetic interpretation of opposing views and an avoidance of wrangling or power plays; this can include a combined effort by all parties to name the arguments for, then the arguments against a particular option. Any choice involves both loss and gain, and we need to be honest about this;
> Prayer, in which one asks to be shown what God wants;
> The testing of a proposed option against the touchstone of faith. As I write, there are strongly opposing views about Pope Francis' programme for the Church. Who is right? Every choice must be in tune with the Gospel imperative of love;
> The experience of consolation and desolation: 'Does this fit well with what we believe? Does it bring true joy?'
> The fruits of the Spirit will characterise communal discernment: love, joy, peace, patience, kindness, generosity, faithfulness, gentleness and self-control (See Galatians 5:22).

 The People of God have a major role to play in discerning how the Church should move forward.

III. OPEN TO THE SPIRIT

The Spirit is always at work, trying to speak to the heart of every person. Without the Holy Spirit there is no 'rumour of angels'. The following reflection paints in stark colours the qualitative difference at meetings when we try to be open to the Holy Spirit. The choice is ours.

> *Without the Holy Spirit, God is far away, Christ stays in the past, the Gospel is a dead letter, the Church is simply an organisation, authority is a matter of domination, mission a matter of propaganda, the Liturgy no more than an evocation, Christian living a slave morality ...*
>
> *But in the Holy Spirit the cosmos is resurrected and groans with the birth-pangs of the Kingdom, the Risen Christ is here, the Gospel is the power of life, the Church shows forth the life of the Trinity, authority is a liberating service, mission is a Pentecost, the Liturgy is both memorial and anticipation, and human action is deified.*
>
> Ignatios of Latakia,
> *Address to the World Council of Churches*, 1968

GRACEFUL WRESTLING

In the presence of the Holy Spirit, heated debate is transformed into a prayerful exploration of the mind of God. Participants wrestle gracefully with one another, share insights on what God may wish, and trust God to move their hearts to what is best. After a settling exercise, a short period of prayer can focus the group's awareness of the Spirit. Such a prayer might run as follows:

> *God, we ask you to bless us as we begin our work. You have been here before us, you wait for us. May your Spirit be welcome in*

this group and enlighten us so that we make good decisions.
Help us to recognise your beckoning through what we share with
one another. While we each have some little wisdom, help us to
remember that you are the primary wisdom figure among us.

'Who speaks for wolf?' The invitation to act as spokesperson for the Spirit is awe-inspiring and challenging, but it is hugely important. This is the challenge which God set the Jews: as a Chosen People, they were to shape their whole lives and make all their decisions in line with God's project. Saint Paul tells Christians to shape each aspect of their lives in harmony with the single law of Love (Romans 12; 1 Corinthians 13). This call is both individual and communal.

For St Paul, there is an intimate relationship between yourself and the Holy Spirit, because the Spirit is already in residence in the depths of your heart. You don't have to evoke the Spirit from some distant place in the sky or even from the local church. All you need to do is to get in touch with your own heart. The Spirit is inside, not out there somewhere. When your spirit and the Spirit of God are in harmony, you can operate out of that harmony. This is what makes the experience of true consolation so important. Imagine the Spirit as managing the Sat Nav of your heart as previously mentioned. Attend to it: ask for eyes to see, ears to hear. Then you'll have confidence at every turn of your journey, no matter where it is taking you.

When you engage in group or communal discernment you take on the role of a searcher. You have to ask the right questions and be a good listener. There is little place in communal discernment for the self-assured – in the *Magnificat*, the so-called 'rich' are sent empty away. Discerners need to be persons of prayer, and to ask for a wisdom not their own. 'God, give me the wisdom that sits by your throne, that she may labour at my side, and that I may learn what is pleasing to you. For she knows and understands all things, and she will guide me wisely in my actions' (see Chapter 9 of Wisdom of Solomon).

LET EVERYONE BE HEARD!

In discerning, we must read the signs of the present times rather than fixate on the past. New wine, new wineskins! We need radical fidelity to Gospel values to see how the world can best be served. Decision-makers need to be in touch: they need to know the facts, from experience rather than from theory. What can celibates say about family life that a group of married people would not say much better? What can the comfortable say about a poor Church? The poor would say it better.

So a Roman synod on the family should have a strong representation of those living family life in its various forms. These people would work with the bishops to produce agreed guidelines regarding family life.

Likewise, in regard to the full participation of women in the decision-making processes of the Church. The pope wants this, even if he is not getting too far on it. The voice of women is as important as the voice of men; the Holy Spirit has worked through them – Our Lady, Elizabeth, Mary of Bethany, Mary of Magdala ... We must take hope from the fact that over the centuries the Church has changed its stance on many things in our own times. Vatican II took a fresh approach to ecumenics, non-Christian religions, freedom of conscience, the role of the Church in the world, the use of vernacular languages. The time is already overdue for the issue of women in the Church to be discerned gracefully. This would involve a prayerful and respectful atmosphere, in which participants – including women – could share what they believe, and try to notice how God is drawing the Church. In communal discernment there are no winners and losers, only a graced consensus of what God wants us to do right now.

Inner freedom is the key challenge. According to St John, 'The wind blows where it chooses. So it is with everyone who is born of the Spirit'. The wind has no fixed positions, nor should we. We need open minds, though not empty ones. If people say of me, 'He was true to form!' that's not a commendation but a statement that

I have a one-track mind. If I think, 'You can't tell me anything about this' I'm outside the realm of discernment! I need to watch myself, and instead of being bored or irritated by the slowness of others in catching on to what I happen to think is the truth, I have to try to notice where the Spirit may be drawing them, for the Spirit is no respecter of persons. Instead of downing others, I must try to put a good interpretation on what they say. I may disagree, but first I must be open to persuasion, otherwise I am disengaged from the discernment process. 'God is drawn to the humble and contrite of spirit, who tremble at his word' (Isaiah 66:2). Do I tremble so?

 With God we can do great things. We are to let the Spirit preside over the councils of our hearts.

 # SOCIAL DECISION-MAKING

I. WHAT CAN YOU APPEAL TO?

Sharon Latour, an American in public office on the West Coast remarks,

> *It might be that all the elements needed for good discernment are precisely what the world always needs reminding about: slow down ... listen ... digest what you see from the other's perspective ... slow down some more ... remember your history ...*

Group work helps to create a space where people can speak their truth and hope to be heard and respected. When you get to understand the dynamics of social decision-making, you may be able to use some of them even in unpromising situations.

➤ You can appeal to the reasonableness that operates in most persons. Most people want well-run meetings. Early on you might suggest a few basic ground rules, e.g. 'I suggest that everyone gets to speak once before anyone speaks a second time; and that we don't interrupt one another ... What about a two-minute limit for each intervention? ... Can we check out whether everyone feels they have been fairly heard? ... We've been talking hard for the past while: suppose we take time out to draw breath?'

➤ You can use the dynamics of community-building: 'Genuine community of sorts can be established in a few hours when the group is instructed from the outset (1) to refrain from generalisations, (2) to speak personally, (3) to be vulnerable, (4) to avoid attempting to heal or convert, (5) to empty itself [of rigid positions], (6) to listen wholeheartedly and (7) to embrace the painful as well as the pleasant' (M. Scott Peck, *The Different Drum*, Touchstone, 1998). There is plenty to work on in the seven points listed here!

➢ In your own small way you can promote an atmosphere of respect. You do it by showing respect for all, including the off-putting person whom you may not agree with. This encourages others to show respect too. You can signal to people that you have heard them. Then they can relax and perhaps listen themselves.

➢ You can stand for truth. You do it by asking searching questions about the core issues, and by asking that all facts be put on the table. You can 'tell it like it is' when the spirit in the group is going sour. You can name the blocks, neuralgic points and blind spots that are floating around. You can highlight the contributions from those who have integrity and vision. You can propose the strengthening of the group. 'Why don't we ask X to come to our next meeting?'

➢ You may be able to point to Jesus as a man who made tough decisions, stood up for the oppressed, loved people, and gave his life for what he believed in. Even if you can't mention his name, you can portray his values.

➢ You might name the special gifts of some participants. This helps 'soft individualism' to emerge – people become more open to one another. By being a calm centre you can help the group to slow down and make cool decisions after the heat of battle. Your humour will help to reduce tension.

➢ If the group is unwieldy, you might propose that representatives be chosen from among the members, who will report back regularly. Of course, they might delegate *you* ...!

➢ You can use images that bring people out of their tunnel vision. You can remind them of past situations, and with them envision a better future. You can brainstorm to loosen the paralysing grip of a single idea. You can help to clarify the options. You can appeal to values. 'When we were elected we promised to stand with the unemployed. Let's not lose sight of that now!'

➢ You can name the mood of the group. 'We seem to have a lot of energy around this idea!' or instead, 'I feel we're getting bogged down. Are we losing our way?'

➢ You can work towards the reasonable choice of an option, and push for a clear process of implementation. By stating what is going on in yourself you can help others get in touch with their feelings and convictions. 'I feel good about this, even though it will make demands on us.' 'How can I convince my wife that this was the right choice?'

Review: What strategies do you feel *you* can use in social decision-making?

YOUR COMMENTS

_____

_____

_____

_____

_____

_____

 In our age, the road to holiness necessarily passes through the world of action.

II. PROTESTING THE WAR

Recall that we are using the term **social decision-making** to cover a situation where an *individual* is trying to use the dynamics of discernment in a group that may not be explicitly involving God in their efforts. There follow two examples.

I went to study in New York in 1969, when the Vietnam War was at its height. On Sundays I worked in a Long Island parish and sometimes spoke against it from the pulpit. But this split the congregation: I was accused of using my position to meddle in political and military affairs. The Chair of the Parish Pastoral Council decided to hold a meeting to resolve the tension, which was running high, and, on Pentecost Sunday 1971, a group gathered in the leafy Church grounds. The chairperson stated that there was one rule: that we should speak respectfully of one another. She added that if disrespect was shown, she would clap her hands: we would then stand and recite together the Our Father.

I was invited to speak first, so I set out briefly the Church's position about war. Some people clapped. Then a big man with a sombrero stood up and addressed us. 'My friends,' he said, 'we know how Communism has spread behind the Iron Curtain. But it has infected many countries in Western Europe too. It can even be found under strange and appealing disguises within our own borders, and when we detect it, we must act against it. So what I will do is take off my hat and pass it around this gathering. Please donate generously so that we will have enough to buy an air ticket for Fr Grogan, to send him back to the country from which he came.'

There was a moment of frozen silence, then the chair clapped her hands, stood up and yelled out the Our Father. The meeting ended abruptly.

I learned a few lessons that day! The idea of meeting to discuss a neuralgic issue was in itself good. But the opposing sides needed to find common ground – such as the Church's attitude to Communism and Jesus' critique of violence – before setting out their stalls for or against the war. Jumping into the cauldron without some preparation was disastrous. Inner freedom was minimal: I should have acknowledged the well-intentioned efforts of the US and the sacrifices made by its fifty-thousand dead American troops. I needed to win goodwill by admitting the threat which Communism presented to the world at that time. Social decision-making is hard going and demands lots of preparation! It is not work for the faint-hearted.

III. CHRISTIANS AND MUSLIMS

Imagine a parish meeting called by your Parish Pastoral Council. The topic is how to respond to the recent development of an Islamic community within the parish. Imagine also that you have decided to attend. You have the background already given in this book. This parish group is good-willed, but it is focused on its problem rather than on God. You have heard some worrying remarks in the shopping centre about friction already emerging between some Muslims and their Catholic counterparts.

Your attitudes of mind and heart are important. Are you going to this meeting as an independent person, or as an ambassador for the Holy Spirit (2 Corinthians 5:20)? Are you praying to be given the words you need? Do you sense yourself in touch with God?

Do you see yourself as a listening post – listening to others but also to 'what the Spirit is saying to the church' (see Revelation 2:29)? Are you asking yourself, 'What is God's view here?' Do you believe that since God's goal is the development of community among us all, there are divine preferences, and that God will be trying to work on the hearts of the participants, including yours? Do you sense some energy in yourself that might in fact be coming from 'above'?

The meeting gets off to a poor start. No background is presented that would point up the common ground that exists between Christians and Muslims. There is no reference to the positive approach to Islam to which Catholics are called since Vatican II – that would have helped to soften the atmosphere. The Chair invites comments from the floor. Most speakers are perturbed by some recent global developments, citing, in particular, recent atrocities by jihadist extremists. You are trying to maintain an open stance, but it's hard. In fact you find yourself in agreement with much of what is being said. What to do?

Having sent off a prayer to the Holy Spirit, you try to express the mood in the hall, in the hope that the truth sets us free (John 8:32). So you say, 'I'm hearing a good deal of fear tonight, and I sympathise with those who have spoken over the past forty-five minutes. Could we break for a few minutes to get in touch with what's going on in us and then look at what God might want us to do?'

When the meeting resumes the chair invites those who have been silent so far to speak. The pause seems to have brought a bit of calm to the proceedings. You observe that while before the break the strident were pushing their own ideas, now others are coming in tentatively, and their interventions have the ring of humility. You wonder if they are perhaps trying to attend to the whispers of the Spirit. This jolts you into asking yourself if you too should be listening to another voice while attending to what is going on. The question hits you: 'Am I meant to be speaking for wolf?' You make another urgent prayer for divine help and plunge in, catching up the fresh dynamic of the group. You might say, 'I was impressed by the line the last two speakers are taking – that we need to do some background work if we're to understand this emerging situation. I know very little about Islam or its beliefs, and I don't know much about the Church's efforts to interact with Islam. I vaguely remember that Vatican II said something positive about it, which apparently was a surprise at the time. I wonder what God would want us to do?'

Silence falls – you can feel it. Then the Chair says, 'Have you a proposal?' So it's back to you. 'Well, could we plan an information evening about Islam? I'd be willing to help organise it. Others might also. We need to find a speaker who knows how the Church has consolidated relationships with its Muslim neighbours in other communities. The chair asks the two priests, yourself and whoever else is willing to stay behind to form a working group, and then brings the meeting to an end. You go home, wondering what you have let yourself in for!

 The Lord entrusts us with the mission of actively participating in everything that enhances the dignity of the daughters and sons of God.

Pope Francis

COMMUNAL DECISION-MAKING

I. HOW THE JESUITS CAME TO BE

The dynamics of communal decision-making are clearly set out in an event which occurred in Rome in Spring 1539. This event became known as the *Deliberation of the First Jesuits*. Its outcome made a significant impact on the world and the Church because it led to the foundation of the Jesuits, whose constitutions and ways of proceeding influenced the formation of later congregations. But even more importantly, after Vatican II and the effort by religious congregations to return to their life-giving sources, it became the seminal document for the reinterpretation of group discernment in our times. For the text see J.C. Futrell SJ: *Making an Apostolic Community of Love* (St Louis, 1970).

BACKGROUND

Over the years previous to the *Deliberation*, the wandering Basque Ignatius of Loyola had gathered a group of nine companions, all of whom wanted to put themselves at God's service. In 1534 they had agreed that they all wanted 'to help others', to serve the Church, to preach in poverty as the apostles did, to work in the Holy Land if possible, or instead to put themselves at the disposal of the pope. They had planned to go to the Holy Land in 1537, but the Turks controlled the seas, so the ideal of ministering in the Holy Land had to be abandoned. They then decided to activate their decision to put themselves at the pope's service anywhere in the world. It appeared that their long and life-giving relationship with one another was about to terminate through this scattering. They were uncertain that this was what God wanted so they decided to work through the issue to determine God's will.

The details of their deliberation need not detain us long. An understanding of the process of discernment which they used can, however, help us to see how communal discernment can be used flexibly today. How then did they go about their task?

They were set on God: What they shared in common was the earnest desire to find God's preferred way for them to be of service to the Church.

They were clear on the issues: They clarified that the central issues were as follows: 'Should we stay together or dissolve our companionship so as to be freer for service? And if we decide to stay together, should we found a religious order?'

They were self-aware: This was a high-quality group. They were men whose hearts and souls were set on God: they had given up everything in life to be available 'to help others'. They were an exceptional band of friends and had endured much together. They were equals, for although they had made the Spiritual Exercises under Ignatius' guidance, and were bonded together around him, he was not their superior. Now decisions had to be made about the future, and each knew how easily he could be blown off-course by disordered preferences.

They had inner freedom: Their years together and their effort to live out the Spiritual Exercises meant that they had reached a high level of inner freedom. The goal of the Exercises is to help persons to place themselves unreservedly before God and make decisions in freedom in order to please God. They shared their views honestly and independently.

They had high respect for one another: The freedom of each was fully respected. They tried to listen deeply to one another. Each took his turn to imagine that he was a newcomer to the group. This helped them to look at their companionship from an objective rather than a subjective or emotional perspective.

They took the time needed: They set no limit to the process, meeting each evening to share what was coming up for them, after which they planned the next step of the deliberation.

They kept God before their eyes: They committed themselves to consistent prayer. They decided that they would wait for God to show what he wished of them, and would try to notice the movements of consolation and desolation in their hearts in relation to the conflicting options. But they also kept God before their eyes in a down-to-earth way by serving the poor nearby.

They sincerely explored all options: On one day each listed the disadvantages of the option being discussed, and on another day, the advantages. Normally people focus only on the arguments in favour of their own positions. The idea here was that by having all of them focus on the arguments in favour or against an option, they would become freer.

They waited for consensus: The process in fact took three months and concluded with unanimity that they would remain together and have a superior. All committed themselves to these decisions by signing a document to this effect.

They sought confirmation: They wanted to work as a group within the Church, and the pope accepted their request.

They implemented their decision: In 1540, a year after the *Deliberation*, the Society of Jesus was founded, with Ignatius elected as superior general. He had hoped to be free to 'help others' in whatever part of the world to which he might be sent. Instead he spent the remaining sixteen years of his life governing and writing constitutions for the new order. Without this work the society would have been stillborn.

THE OUTCOME

The Society of Jesus blossomed: when Ignatius died there were some one thousand members. Since then it is estimated that there have been some one hundred and sixty-eight thousand Jesuits in all. The first companions never met again as a group; they were missioned across the world directly by the pope, or more ordinarily by their superior who acted according to the mind of the pontiff. But they remained bonded as they had wished, by obedience, by love, by letters and in other ways. This helped to give them 'courage in difficult enterprises' as Ignatius put it.

It is not clear that the *Deliberation of the First Jesuits* was ever repeated in such an intensive way. However, the dynamics remain permanently valid, and any group can adapt it if it wants to take seriously the communal search for the will of God. Likewise, as we have seen in speaking of *social decision-making*, an individual can try to use some of the dynamics of Ignatian discernment at any meeting. As we have seen, Pope Francis has opted for communal discernment, in appropriate forms, to work through the major issues facing the Church today.

 Discernment is the dynamic process of choosing the values of Jesus and of living by the Spirit.

II. A CONGREGATION TRIMS ITS SAILS

By **communal decision-making** we mean that a *group of believers*, faced with a common challenge for decision, is trying to follow the principles of discernment to discover the calling of God in a concrete situation. There follow some examples.

A congregation engaged some years ago in a process of rationalisation. It was running a large number of apostolic works, all with their own impressive history. But the combination of declining numbers, ageing personnel and financial constrictions indicated to them the need to plan *comprehensively* for the future, rather than to limp along by crisis management. The congregation also wanted to secure for its small cohort of younger members the freedom to meet emerging situations rather than to have to maintain outmoded works. They had had no entrants for over a decade and felt that future prospects were bleak.

BUYING IN

Because they themselves had been appointed through a good discernment process, the members of the Congregational Leadership Team (CLT) bought into discernment again, without knowing in detail what it might involve. Note the courage involved in this decision: it would have been easier to drift along, reacting to crises as they emerged, so that, as one member put it, 'we could blame the *situation* for having to close down a work, rather than take the responsibility ourselves'.

The CLT identified a consultant who was familiar with communal discernment, though he had never been involved in a task of this magnitude before. They appointed him as Ministries Planning Consultant. He became known simply as the 'MC'.

The MC proposed that the work would take at least two years. This was agreed, after which the MC interviewed individually as many of the congregation as possible and a number of their key lay colleagues. Confidentiality was assured. Two themes emerged from this initial exercise:

1. A desire to continue the charism of the foundress.
2. A desire for serious and intelligent pruning, despite the pain involved.

With this overall support or 'buy-in' by the stakeholders, the MC submitted a time schedule for the evaluation of each of the current operations. His task was clarified and fine-tuned with the CLT. He would have access to all personnel and to all necessary information; and he would present reports one by one to the CLT. Each report would contain an evaluation of the ministry in question, together with realistic options for the future, and the pros and cons for each. There his task would end: the CLT would take up the work of decision-making and implementation. The CLT would also have to decide whether to implement changes one by one, or wait until all reports were in so that they could evaluate each ministry within a comprehensive overview. Not surprisingly they found themselves obliged to compromise.

CRITERIA

Criteria for the evaluation were drawn from the Constitutions of the Congregation and the Guidelines from the recent Provincial Assembly. Included were:

➢ Fidelity to the founding charism, which was the service of the most needy among the poor. Introduced here was the dimension of advocacy, the supporting of groups which lobby for structural change on behalf of the poor.
➢ Enablement of lay persons who could continue the charism accordingly as the congregation's workforce declined. They called this the 'Multiplier Effect'.

> Care for their ageing personnel, non-overburdening of those currently in the workforce, and liberation of younger members from maintenance so that they could put their unique gifts at service of emerging needs. As they put it, 'We need to minimise the WOW factor – 'Worn Out Workers'!
> Concern for the religious spirit of the group, including growth in relationship with God, supportive community structures, inner happiness and time for one another.
> Best use of limited financial resources, to ensure that priority projects would be sustainable.

In a well-orchestrated series of meetings, these criteria were agreed by an expanded Leadership Team in consultation with congregation members. Already elements of the discernment process were being used – prayerful consideration and attentive listening. A gentle atmosphere developed around a procedure that in itself was painful. One of the spin-offs of the labour of communal discernment soon became evident – a deepened sense of community, expressed in the energising remark, 'We're in this together! No matter what happens, we're more united than we have ever been!'

STILL GENERATIVE
The CLT spent time – not without differing views – on what they wanted from the MC. The more tidy-minded wanted clear and precise proposals which required from them only the task of implementation. They wanted to 'finish' some works, close some non-viable institutions and walk away from impossible burdens. There was a vocal lobby for freedom for those still in the work force, even though it meant the abandonment of things cherished.

Others felt drawn to a more open stance. They felt that orderly 'solutions' in which loose ends are neatly tied up can diminish life rather than enhance it. While the congregation's evaluation was completed before the publication in November 2013 of Pope Francis' *The Joy of the Gospel*, this group would later found support in what he says there:

> *What we need is to give priority to actions which generate new processes in society and engage other persons and groups who can develop them to the point where they bear fruit (n. 223).*

In the Pope's mind, life flows and has an unpredictable quality about it, and so does the Word of God and the action of the Spirit. We can control life by ticking boxes; or we can sow seeds, initiate, and 'work slowly but surely, without being obsessed with immediate results' (n. 223).

The CLT engaged a facilitator for their own meetings to learn how to live with the tensions that arose. They had been appointed to shape the congregation for the future, and this would involve tough choices around terminations. But they came to look to the future from a free space, rather than to control it. They reminded themselves that the future belongs to God, and that they must try to be in tune with the ways God goes about things, rather than the ways they felt drawn to themselves. The divine future might show itself in disconcerting fashion, knocking their planning sideways. Openness to uncertainty was stressful, but they grew closer together in this process and became more tentative and humble. And they grew to admire one another more. They made Thomas Merton's discernment prayer their own:

> *Lord God, we have no idea where we are going. We do not see the road ahead of us. We cannot know for certain where it will end. Nor do we really know ourselves, and the fact that we think that we are following your will does not mean that we are actually doing so. But we believe that the desire to please you does in fact please you. And we hope we have that desire in*

all that we are doing. We hope that we will never do anything apart from that desire. And we know that if we do this you will lead us by the right road though we may know nothing about it. Therefore will we trust you always though we may seem to be lost and in the shadow of death. We will not fear, for you are ever with us, and you will never leave us to face our perils alone.

Thoughts in Solitude, 1956

TELLING THE STORY

The journey of personal adaptation for the future has to begin somewhere, so the CLT decided to begin it by 'telling the story'. This brought everyone on board and gained further common ground, a key factor for the success of communal discernment. They created a 'story line' which indicated where each person had come in, and what had happened along the journey of the congregation. One member summed it up for the group:

> *So this is how it all started: this is what the founding members were trying to do: they sowed seeds for an unknown future. Numbers were tiny, but those first members had extraordinary faith and allowed themselves be led by God. God must have found them easy to manage! There were false beginnings in some situations, but disproportionate fruits in others. Here we see the heights of growth and success, and there are the valleys of darkness. And we can see where each of us came in, and what we each brought to the story. So here we are now, with a deepened sense that God has truly been in our history, and will be as we walk into the future. Should we say it is our story, or God's, or both? Haven't we and God been co-creating?*

Such reflections brought an awed wonder about the activity of divine providence in their history. Courage grew that they were not walking alone – they prayed Psalm 23 about God being with them in the valley of darkness. Also they grew in the *corporate capacity to change and to rationalise*. Humility emerged, the messiah-complex waned, and members came to see themselves as God's servants whose task was to do what the Lord wanted, rather than what they might have wished. They were able to use Simeon's prayer: 'Master, now you are dismissing your servants in peace' (Luke 2:29). All of this eased the labour of the CLT.

Much creativity went into setting up their meetings in ways that facilitated calm, inner freedom, ease of discourse, heart-listening, and spaces for reflection, prayer and liturgy. Décor, chair arrangement, presentation of both sides of each issue all helped, as did comfortable venues and tasty food. Marathon sessions were avoided and the aged and the hard of hearing were discreetly catered for.

THE SIGNS OF THE TIMES

Meanwhile the MC was at work. His task was to read well 'the signs of the times' (Matthew 16:3). This demanded a detailed review of the history and current state of each ministry, how it matched up to the agreed criteria, and its ongoing viability. Past, present and future were inter-linked. Also important was contextualisation: someone said, 'Don't let us be like moles who burrow away underground and rarely come up to see what others are doing!' So they began to look outward, and a new criterion was added: 'Is this work being done well by some other group, religious or lay?' If yes, the option to terminate it or to merge its resources with that other operation was included in the report. Note that the MC's focus was on the apostolate itself. It was not an evaluation of how effectively the assigned members were engaged in it. This eased the fear that anyone would get 'a bad report'.

Consultants immerse themselves in the life-flow of a group as they try to see what is most significant. So, like a detective, the MC mulled over the facts and tried to follow up all leads, even the unpromising. The mass of data was bewildering, and opposing interpretations clamoured for attention. Often he heard the appeal, 'This work would be fine if we had another pair of hands, or an injection of money, or whatever.'

He believed that the Holy Spirit was at work in the seeming chaos, setting things up, sprinkling clues, shedding needed light. He followed the scent of the Spirit through multilayered listening sessions and conversations. St Ignatius' remark in the Jesuit Constitutions on how the Superior General of the Jesuits might spend his day was helpful. 'He should divide his time partly with God, partly with his helpers, and partly with himself in reflecting privately and thinking out and deciding what should be done with the help and favour of God our Lord' (n. 809). The MC found that after a while he was habitually in discernment mode – listening to others, asking God's help, noting the movements of his own heart, trying to maintain objectivity. And the contemplative dimension of the CLT was growing.

REFLECTIVE DISRUPTION

Scharmer & Kaufer's book, *Leading from the Emerging Future* (Berrett-Koehler, 2013) was published just after the congregation's discernment process ended. It is written from a secular perspective – God is mentioned only once! Nevertheless it has resonances of the discernment process. The thesis is that a new world is waiting to emerge, one that will be characterised by healthy relationships rather than by exploitation, individualism, domination, oppression, destructiveness. To reach this goal *reflective* disruption will be required, so that those who currently mishandle the world will stop, realise what they are doing, and come to a new quality of awareness. This would bring about a shift from a selfish view or ego-awareness to what the authors call *eco-system awareness*, which values the well-being of others and the well-being of the planet before personal desires. The journey is from 'me' to 'we'. The success of our decisions, the authors say, depends not so much on what we do or how, *but on the inner place from which we operate.* We need a *transformed quality of attention.* The authors acknowledge contemplative practice as helpful to get in touch with the deeper 'soul' from which we can operate, which, they say, tends to be outside the range of normal awareness.

Contemplative practice is what discernment is all about. The Congregation and especially the CLT were trying to see things from the divine perspective – what God wants to happen in the world. They were trying to avoid the distortions that undermine choices which would better promote the kingdom of God in the here and now. There was no sense of certainty attached to their efforts, but their desire as they laboured through one report after another was clear: they wanted to be in tune with the divine project. And that was surely enough. We may believe that their 'pruning process' will bear its own good fruit (see John 15:2).

 'The divine future may reveal itself in disconcerting fashion, knocking our planning sideways.'

III. CARE FOR THE WORLD

Every day we hear of ordinary people who take up causes that merit media attention. Could this be how the Spirit works to inspire others to 'go and do likewise'? As I write, the story of Malala Yousafzai is again hitting the daily papers. Shot in the head in 2012 by the Taliban while returning home in a school bus in northern Pakistan, she recovered and has become an advocate for universal child education. A Nobel Peace Prize winner in 2014, she has taken on world leaders for their slowness to respond to her challenge of education for all, and is a symbol of what one passionate person can achieve.

My concerns should match those of Jesus. Not that I can do much, but let me be concerned, and make my small contribution as best I can. I may choose to work on the exclusion of women from decision-making processes in the Catholic Church, or on the local poverty situation, or on climate issues. 'What does God want me to do?' This is the recurring question in Ignatian spirituality.

THE QUALITY OF CHRISTIAN ADVOCACY

We look here at the Ignatian Advocacy Network as an instance of communal discernment in action on the global level. Its goals are daring:

> - to build bridges between rich and poor;
> - to link those who exercise political and economic power with those who cannot articulate their own concerns;
> - to create a dialogue between oppressor and oppressed, rather than to shame, hurt, enrage, humiliate. 'Never break the bridge' is an important rule of thumb;
> - to focus power towards the good of the disempowered, so that a fractured world is healed and transformed;
> - to challenge in effective ways unjust laws, policies and practices.

The strategy to achieve these goals is neither arms nor trade embargoes, but a constructive and respectful engagement with those in power. Ideally it means that all parties would sit on the same side of the table and gaze out together at the needs of peoples. Issues include migration, peace and human rights, education, ecology and natural resources, alternative models of sustainable development, religious fundamentalism and overseas development aid.

Take the example of refugees. The Jesuit Refugee Service (JRS) was set up by Pedro Arrupe, Superior General of the Jesuits, in 1980, when he saw the plight of the Vietnamese 'boat people'. He wanted the Jesuit order to be at the service of forcibly displaced persons across the world. Such people now number more than thirty-five million. The task of the JRS is to accompany and serve refugees on the ground, and also to defend them by advocating for them. It uses a hands-on approach that makes heavy physical and emotional demands. Its credibility is enhanced by its grass-root engagement: this is not an armchair advocacy.

The Ignatian motto is 'In all things to love and serve' and this is demanding. What is needed among advocates for any cause is a common vision for the world, a belief that the goods of creation are intended by God for all, and a desire to respond lovingly, compassionately and effectively to an identified need. The ideal for all peoples to live is life to the full (John 10:10). This demands an attitude of contemplation: sitting with God and contemplating God's world, being realistic regarding resources, and using imaginative discernment about when and where to join in the action. Even a small group, when aligned on this vision, can endure frustration and setbacks, yet still accomplish great things.

IGNATIAN ADVOCATES ARE PERSONS WHO ...

➢ Enter into solidarity with the marginalised, and work to empower them to become subjects rather than objects of their own history;

> Are marked by inner freedom. They try to purify their motivation from rage, compulsion, need for success and approval, ego-flattery, self-will. They ask themselves if they are unknowingly complicit in injustice, and if so, they try to change. They need passion and enthusiasm, but without inner discernment they will end up hating or despising the oppressors;
> Try to be contemplatives in action, relying on God to lead them in the task of creating right relations and reconciling differences;
> Discern the deep feelings and desires of their hearts to see which are truly life-giving to those they serve;
> Engage with the structures of power and decision-making in a relational manner. They have high ideals but are pragmatic enough to take even tiny steps forward;
> Are adaptable, creative and responsive, intellectually rigorous and competent, loving and world-affirming;
> Proceed by communal discernment, are open to partnership with anyone of good will, and always seek to be of greater service.

The very act of being with the oppressed and the needy is already a step towards community, which is God's unwavering desire. Even if no significant change of circumstances occurs, the development of good relationships and of solidarity is a blessing, because community is itself an intrinsic value. If their joy depended on success, they would often be unhappy. The joy must be in the doing. Advocacy is not only an issue-based process, it is self-implicating: advocates are changed by their own involvement. Solidarity with the poor comes at a cost, which can include suffering, frustration, loss, dispossession and even death. Jesus sided with the poor, suffered and was killed because of his efforts to transform relationships between the mighty and the lowly.

 The development of good relationships and solidarity with the needy is a blessing.

SEEKING AND FINDING GOD

If a group tries to keep God in view, its meetings will be characterised by a contemplative quality rather than by human busyness and bright ideas. Qualities such as the following will be found:

Searching: The term 'contemplation' essentially refers to the 'God-quality'. In contemplation one is searching for God. Walter Burghardt describes contemplation as 'taking a long, loving look at the real' – we gaze on things with God's eyes and see what God may want done. Each member tries to help the others to find God in the issue at hand, rather than to promote their own agenda.

Waiting: God is acknowledged as the point of reference: the group waits prayerfully for *God* to show what is to be done, as opposed to saying: 'Let's get this sorted out fast!' or 'That's a great idea – it will sort out our financial problems!' An atmosphere of prayer and sensitivity to God's values prevails.

God taking over: Contemplation involves the experience of God 'making his presence felt'. This may be a 'wow' experience, or the quiet but consoling conviction that this or that is what God wants done, a sense that the touch of God is in one option rather than another. Only when God intervenes does the group move forward. Joy, peace and energy follow when the members sense that they have 'news of God!'

Group Development can help a gathering of believers to become co-workers with God. Such development requires:

> ➢ A commitment to the process of becoming a discerning group.
> ➢ A willingness by each to share their (limited) sense of God, so that a group sense of God may emerge, that is, the group's conviction that it is limitlessly loved by God, and that God is inviting the members to work together with the Spirit to make human history better.
> ➢ A humility that allows each to admit their prejudices and to let go of cherished projects; to speak out honestly, not in anger but in love; to face change with courage, to listen well and to accept others as they are.
> ➢ A capacity to build on the group's strengths and limits. Each one is implicitly saying to the others, 'I am here for you. I don't want to get my way. I want to serve you by listening well, by praying, and by contributing whatever wisdom I have.'
> ➢ An authenticity born of prayer and listening out for the Spirit, so that each contribution emerges out of a depth that is beyond the merely human. The discernment is only as good as the personal purification and liberty of each involved. This requires authentic, no-nonsense prayer.

The power and resilience of such a group can be amazing; it can weather opposition, frustration, and disappointments because it is founded on rock (see Luke 6:48). That rock is the Lord. As the group works its way along, discipleship deepens imperceptibly in each of the members, and decisions get made with greater spontaneity. The Spirit can work freely through unexpected twists and turns which may seem like reversals, but which in fact help the advancement of the Kingdom of God.

CONSOLATION

It is certainly vital for advocates to learn the context and the facts, to move from experience to analysis, and from analysis to reflection and to prayer; then to priorities, action and evaluation. But time is often limited, situations can change with bewildering speed, and fresh decisions become urgent. Often the best a group can do is to say, 'This seems the best thing to do right now; in the name of God let's try it.' Perhaps the new initiative will fail miserably or be overwhelmed by a new disaster. As the saying goes, 'It is small comfort when you're surrounded by alligators, to protest that all you wanted to do was to drain the swamp!' How can a group remain in consolation in such a situation?

> The primary consolation for human beings lies in Christian revelation, which proclaims the limitless love of God for the world, Jesus' radical victory over sin and death, the command to witness to the Kingdom of God, and the promise of everlasting joy for all humankind.
> This revelation gives unshakeable confidence that the world we love and the people we serve are in good hands, no matter how much they may be enduring now.
> Solidarity with the oppressed of the earth demands self-transcendence: but this brings us close to God, and therefore to consolation. God thus rewards those who fall in love with the poor. We become in a new way 'the blessed of God' (Matthew 25:34). It is a good thing to sympathise with Jesus on the Cross, but we move to another level when we ask, 'How can we help to get the crucified persons of the world off their crosses today?'
> Acceptance by those we serve brings joy. They reveal God's presence by their capacity to celebrate life even in the midst of appalling misery.
> Consolation comes essentially from God rather than from human achievement. It saves us from being depressed when things are bad, because it is born of belief that Jesus carries our burdens and that his light shines in the darkness of our surroundings, and that this light 'cannot be overcome' (John 1:5).

When a group is set on God, the Spirit can work freely through unexpected twists and turns which may seem like reversals, but which in fact help the advancement of the Kingdom of God.

SUMMARY OF THE DYNAMICS OF COMMUNAL DISCERNMENT

The process of communal discernment is a transparent one. Nothing is intentionally hidden by the members from one another. The group can rely on the inherent graced quality of what goes on, because the process is centred on God who is understood to be fully engaged in it. The following elements are involved in formal group discernment, while less formal discernment will involve an appropriate choice of elements as the situation allows.

Composing the group: Who should be a member? And how are members to be appointed? The members need not be 'yes' people: groups make better progress when healthy tension exists. Capacity to work well together is what matters, and a willingness to engage in searching together for the desire of God. The God of decision-making is a communicating God; the group wants to interpret the divine language as best it can. Good leadership is essential; leadership skill training can help the whole group.

From group to community: The socialisation and faith formation of the group is vital if the it is to become cohesive and effective. Sharing of personal, human and faith stories builds common appreciation. Likewise how each feels in their new role is important, as are their values, images of God, vision for Church, and special concerns. Exercises that foster awareness of the gifts within the group build confidence, as does the humble acknowledgement of limitations. The group must be weak enough to realise that the success of its work depends on God rather than on the members.

Ongoing development: The care of the group is often neglected, but without appropriate care a group will gradually weaken. Shared events such as parties, outings, retreat days, faith formation and skills updating, all help.

Inner freedom: We come to meetings with our contrasting styles, with unclarified assumptions, biases and prejudices. This is normal: the skill is to try to acknowledge such realities, otherwise they put the discernment process off course. We all limp and have limited vision: only when we are aware can we compensate effectively. Then we can come into the open with our hidden agendas and lean on the strengths of others, and especially on the strength of God.

Shared vision: 'Unless the people have vision, they perish.' Vision is a dynamic that must adjust to the changes which are constant in human living. Is there a shared vision of Church? How does the group see its power? Is power shared? Are roles clear? Is the group consultative? Does it relate with parallel groupings?

Process: A facilitator can be helpful, and the chair must be competent for the task of the group. Brady and Grogan's *Meetings Matter* (Veritas, 2009) provides material to help all members know what they are meant to be about. Preparation of the meeting, a concise agenda, and a capacity to see discussion through to decisions are important.

Prayer: An atmosphere of prayer must prevail: not simply rushed vocal prayer, but silent time too. Throughout, the group tries to keep God in view and to test options against the Gospels and its own mission statement.

Topic: For concreteness, let us suppose that the group has gathered because it wants to respond to Pope Francis' call to all Christians to become 'evangelisers'. Someone introduces *The Joy of the Gospel*, which has already been distributed with encouragement to read it. A general chat might follow, to bring everyone up to speed: 'Did anyone get through it all?' 'Did you find it easy to read?' 'Was it off-putting?'

Brainstorming: This opens up the world of possibilities we spoke of at the beginning of this book. 'Should we go through it slowly and methodically, or take the section about parishes and work out from there?' 'Is there another parish which has already taken up the document?' 'Let's start by reviewing all we are already doing about evangelising.' The group begins to claim its voice, gaining courage and a sense of solidarity.

Listening: The group may need training in listening skills. Everyone must have a chance to speak, and interventions should be tentative rather than dogmatic; no monopolising of the microphone; no interruptions. Respect includes putting a good interpretation on others' statements; asking for clarification. 'Have I understood you rightly about this?' Sensitive chairing and positive comments help.

Data: After several meetings, perhaps parish involvement is proposed. Then a survey may be required, also financial data, interested parties, history of similar ventures, etc.

Clarification of options: 'Shall we work with *The Joy of the Gospel*? If yes, let's decide how to tackle it.'

The light of the Gospel: 'What word or scene helps here?' 'What values of Jesus will be found in this option?' Members may be able to test the option against previous experiences of the presence of God in their hearts.

For and Against: If the option is divisive, all could work together on the 'reasons for', then on the 'reasons against'. This frees the members from defending their preferred options, and brings an increased sense of common purpose.

Waiting for consolation: In silent prayer, each asks again for inner freedom. 'Lord, save us from our prejudices and biases! Let what pleases you be done.' Each tries to notice the nudging of the Spirit, and in what direction they are being drawn. Consolation will bring a sense of authenticity, rightness, energy, unity, life, love and courage. Desolation brings the opposite.

Consensus: Each person reports to the others what they find going on within themselves: 'Before God, this or that is what I believe we should do.' Consensus begins to emerge. But it is important to listen to 'the other side' – what can be learned from those who are not at ease? The incorporation of some of their concerns may lead the group close to unanimity. The *kairos* (right) moment is when, after long debate and prayer, the participants raise their weary hands to commit themselves to an issue. Then, as a participant at such a meeting said, 'It was as if the room were set on fire with passion for the cause and for the plan.'

Confirmation: The decision may have to be submitted to a higher authority. Beyond that, the members need to look for a continued sense of consolation in themselves regarding the option chosen.

Implementation: Without well-planned implementation, the decision will falter. Generosity will be required of the members to take on the needed tasks.

 The complexities of group decision-making call for a range of wisdom, experience and grace that can be found only in a group.

 **APPENDICES**

I.   A PARISH LETS GOD TAKE CHARGE

Here is a concrete account of how a parish selected a new Parish Pastoral Council (PPC) by a process of communal discernment. It is written by a member of the outgoing PPC.

'A lot had to do with the way our meetings had tended to go. Some people were vocal and opinionated – the loudest voice tended to prevail. We saw that the issue was not to silence vocal persons, but to find a way to get everyone equally involved. I came across a book called *Quiet: The Power of Introverts in a World that Can't Stop Talking*, by Susan Cain. Her argument is that too often we undervalue the contribution of quieter, more reflective persons, and this is everyone's loss. Everyone needs to enter their quiet zone and speak from there. Otherwise their contributions tend to be superficial.'

'I put this tentatively to the parish priest to the PPC. They were interested. They wanted to know how we might get to this place of corporate quiet. I knew something about the discernment process and explained it. We researched it further, presented it to the parish, and then got it going!'

'So we decided that our new PPC should be chosen by communal discernment. Crucially, the process was linked to our parish faith journey from Lent, through Easter, to Pentecost. This brought to life our general understanding of prayerful discernment as 'letting God take charge'! Of course we had to trust the process. Our hidden fear was that if the

Holy Spirit was left to do the choosing of the new team, some unsuitable members might be brought on board. I have often wondered what the Holy Spirit thought about that!'

So, what did they do, and why, and how did it all turn out?

OUR PARISH DISCERNMENT PROCESS

Stage 1: Engagement of the Parish in Prayer, Reflection & Discernment

On the First Sunday of Lent our process began. PPC members spoke at each of the Masses and a booklet detailing the process and timeline was distributed. The four key features communicated at this stage were:

> - *gratitude* to parishioners for their current involvement in our parish and our liturgies;
> - *information* around the role, duty and responsibilities of the PPC, the balance of skills and experience required and the types of people sought. The primary emphasis was that new members should have an interest in faith and the Church, be willing to rely on the Holy Spirit and be guided by Gospel values;
> - *invitation* to all to prayerfully reflect on their possible involvement in the new PPC;
> - *communal prayer* (more on this below). A Prayer of the Faithful each Sunday made a connection between our ongoing discernment and the Gospel theme of the day.

Stage 2: Information Meetings

We held two Information Meetings, open to anyone who wished to consider becoming a member of the incoming PPC. They were led by an outside facilitator and their purpose was threefold;

1. *to engage*: to engage prospective members in facilitated, prayerful discernment;

2. *to inform*: to ensure that those who came were fully informed about the roles and responsibilities relating to the PPC, through dialogue with the outgoing PPC;
3. *to encourage*: to distribute Application Forms, at the meeting's close, to those who wished to proceed in the process.

Stage 3: Application Period

A three week application period commenced after the first meeting. People could be nominated if they allowed their names to go forward. Completed forms were accepted from anyone who had attended one of the two Information Meetings. The forms were submitted directly to the PP/Administrator, President of the PPC. As it turned out, we had to hold our nerve when only a small number initially applied!

Stage 4: Selection of New Parish Pastoral Council

A week later we held our parish AGM. The underlying theme of the meeting was that we would let God take charge. The stages of this facilitated and prayerful session were as follows:

➢ Those who had submitted their names were invited to take the vacated seats of the outgoing PPC;
➢ Each briefly addressed the parish members on their experience and skills, and on what they hoped to bring to the PPC, if chosen;
➢ After a prayer-filled silence those present marked their selection silently on paper. Votes were counted, and the names of those chosen were announced. Appropriately, on Pentecost Sunday they were commissioned and blessed.

REFLECTION ON THE PROCESS

The Information Meetings were crucial and were facilitated to include prayerful reflection on the following themes:

➢ *Learning:* What is discernment? 'Letting God take charge!'
➢ *Petition:* Asking the Holy Spirit to guide our hearts. 'Direct us, Lord, as you see best.'

> *Listening:* Quiet moments to listen to God. As Elijah learned on the mountain, the Lord is not in the mighty wind, nor the earthquake, nor the fire, but in the sound of sheer silence (see 1 Kings 19:11-12).
> *Sharing:* how each person felt drawn by God – without any response from others.

Similarly, the broader meeting of the parish AGM was conducted in an atmosphere of that reflective contemplation which the process, at its best, demands. By 'contemplation' I refer to that steady searching for God, which demands patience, and also sensitivity to the gentle nudging of the Spirit on one's heart.

PRAYER!

Key among the critical learning outcomes was **the importance of prayer**. Prayer permeated the process at every point. It meant that we wanted God to be in charge. It was helpful to link the process to the faith journey of the parish during the liturgical season; to encourage private prayer and reflection; to ensure communal prayer through the discernment meetings and the prayer of the faithful each Sunday; to write a parish discernment prayer – then pray it and publicise it – in the weekly newsletter, on the parish website, on church noticeboards and church banners. Our simple prayer ran as follows:

> *God, our loving Father, guide our hearts and minds as we come*
> *to discern and form our new Parish Pastoral Council. May we*
> *work together to build our parish into a vibrant welcoming*
> *community that reflects the gospel values of love, justice and*
> *peace. We ask this through Christ our Lord. Amen.*

REFLECTIONS ON THE PROCESS

Inclusion: The process was highly inclusive of the entire evolving parish community. This helped to ensure that the parish would not become 'a useless structure, out of touch with people or a self-absorbed cluster made up of a chosen few' (Pope Francis, *The Joy of the Gospel*, 28). The needs of the parish and the gifts of its members became central rather than any individual's popularity or prominence.

Formation: The process provided parish formation on the role of the PPC and pastoral planning generally. Parish planning was to be in line with divine planning: 'We want to do what God wishes: we want God's kingdom to come!' The fact that it was a clearly open and transparent process brought us a new sense of truth and freedom, and a real pride in our parish as being close to God's heart.

God at the Centre: The group respected the decision-making gift of each individual within the PPC, and opened up space for the eternal dance of the Trinity 'through which our parish lives and moves and has its being' (see Acts 17:28). The fear that some 'unsuitable' people might be chosen yielded to a recognition that groups can make better progress when healthy tensions exist: the capacity to work professionally well together is what matters. The spirit of prayer takes care of the rest and bonds the participants together.

A sincere desire to find what God wants done is the foundation of communal discernment. Here it emerged from the strong faith life of the parish. The members wanted to be in tune with God because they recognized that God loves them, cares about them, and wants to work with them. They saw that the 'will of God' is not a static blueprint but an open plan, and that God respected their choices and shaped the parish through them.

Good Listening: Believing that the Spirit is active within the group, each member is now trying to 'tune in' to the divine frequency. The Spirit succeeds in communicating when there is a good level of mutual listening. The Spirit speaks through God's Word, through the members, through careful reading of 'the signs of the times' in the changing contours of the parish, and through the divine tugs on their own hearts. They believe that God provides for a group the resources it needs.

Inner Freedom: If members practise personal discernment, they find the demands of group discernment easier. They are able to challenge one another respectfully so that group freedom is enhanced and openness to the common good is achieved. Hidden agendas can be brought to light or quietly left aside. The disposition of inner freedom means that one's heart is to be 'like a balance at equilibrium' (*Exercises*, 15); and that the love that moves us to one option or another should come not from some selfish desire but 'from above' - that is, from God (*Exercises*, 184). The members try to avoid making up their minds until the last minute, because it is God's privilege to move hearts 'in the fullness of time' (Galatians 4:4). This strategy can be called The Uncertainty Principle'! It offsets the problem that good people can go into meetings with their minds made up beforehand.

Clarity around the Facts: The organising group had to put time, energy and money into reviewing the changing reality of the parish; what the PPC could be at its best; the nature of a discernment process; and how to tailor-make a good selection process for their parish. Gathering and presenting the facts can be laborious; it may demand surveys, provoke disagreement, demand compromises, etc. We need not lose heart since we are dealing with God's world and God's project rather than our own. God is an enabling God!

Consolation and Desolation: There is a corporate dimension now to the experiences of consolation and desolation. These experiences are embedded in the history of the parish, in its vision and mission, its good and bad times, its successes and failures. God is the Lord of our history, and grace is incarnate in every story. So the group can ask: 'Where were we truly at our best?' When it has identified this experience of consolation, it can measure the proposed option against it. Then the question is, 'Does this proposed option harmonise with those times when we were most authentic? Remember when we had energy, enthusiasm, commitment, peace, joy, and a willingness to make sacrifices: will this option renew these qualities?'

Letting God Take Charge! A discerning group must keep God before their eyes. This parish group believed that prayer made a difference, and it did! The members moved easily into silence. They knew that discernment is a contemplative process: that it was their task to prepare and dispose themselves and to beg God to show them what best to do. Each had to wait for the others to reveal what was going on inside their hearts. They shared humbly. One applicant for the PPC said, 'When I prayed about the young man who wanted to follow Jesus but couldn't let go of his riches, a strange sense of joy came to me about letting go of my little securities and privacies. I felt nudged to take this risk.' Another said, 'I was reluctant to go forward, but I couldn't get away from Jesus' words, that what we do for others we do for him.' God's grace played gently in each heart: no-one was under pressure. Those who finally became members of the new PPC felt that they had been chosen. One woman commented: 'Now I know what Jesus meant by saying that he chooses us: I felt it wasn't the priest nor the outgoing members. Of course I was voted in but the atmosphere of prayer made me feel that the voters were letting the Holy Spirit do the work!'

Gospel Criteria: Gospel criteria played an important role. The planners had to ask, 'Will this discernment process help our parish better to serve the kingdom of God?' Those thinking of applying to join the PPC were asked, 'Do you feel that working on the PPC fits in with your sense of being a disciple of Jesus?' Such questions led to deeper questions such as 'What is the kingdom of God about anyhow?' 'What does real discipleship entail? ' One spin-off was that everyone involved came to see a little more clearly what Christian life is about. The process was a down-to-earth experience of adult faith formation.

Deepening of Community: No process is infallible, but when a group sincerely works with the right dispositions, it can say, 'We did our best, and we'd be willing to change our decision if we came to see that it wasn't in fact the wisest and most loving thing to do.' No matter how decisions go, when they are made along lines similar to the above they build community among the members, and in the wider group.

VOICE OF THE PEOPLE

How helpful was the process within the parish? Here are some comments:

> *The parish discernment brought parish members together, with our doubts and our beliefs, and it helped me to see myself as a 'normal' parish member. The process made us aware of the presence of the Spirit. This helped us to make decisions – about application and voting – based on what was good for the parish community. It was a down-to-earth process, church in action, and those of us who were chosen to serve on the PPC felt supported by the parish community.*

> *It was initially through the booklet on the Discernment Process that I felt the stirring of the Holy Spirit within me. I was drawn to engage with the process as it felt that it was the Holy Spirit who was running it and that I could trust the outcome, no matter what it was.*

Personally I felt that the discernment process was a great success. We now have a PPC made up of people who might not otherwise have put themselves forward for election or been strongly involved in the parish. These bring different viewpoints to the meetings – the perspective of a newcomer to the parish or another whose only involvement was attendance at Mass. We have new ideas and fresh enthusiasm. The process encouraged people to reflect on their talents and expertise and how the parish could benefit from their experience.
I fully support the discernment process. It was a well-prepared enterprise with an informative published document and support from the altar by our priest. I recommend it as the way for our diocese in the future.

The booklet played a significant role in helping me to put myself forward as the process laid out in it facilitated my thinking. Having recently retired I had spare time and wanted to offer it to the parish where I grew up. I felt that serving on the Council would give me a different perspective on the parish. So far it has been a rewarding experience.

The image I have of the new PPC is that each of our meetings is to be a little Pentecost. The Holy Spirit is at the centre, and also in each heart. We name and invoke the Spirit. We can press the pause button in the middle of a meeting, to rest with the Spirit for a few minutes. This helps to slow us down, and gives space for God to take charge.

 The well-being of the Church and of the world lies in good decision-making.

II. A THREE-HOUR COMMUNAL DISCERNMENT

INTRODUCTION

A busy parish had been debating an important project for some time. The Parish Pastoral Council members were unsure about it; the finance committee was in favour; the parish priest was keen to go ahead, but the Bishop was cautious, due to the cost involved.

I was asked to facilitate a discernment process between the two groups. I was given three hours, no more, because of time restrictions on the twenty participants. This is my account of what happened. Others perhaps saw it differently. In the days before the meeting I prayed a good deal about it, and gathered up prayer support from various sources, including the parish community. This helped to steady my nerves!

BEGINNINGS

We met at 09.30 a.m. for 10 a.m. in a large airy room; chairs in a circle; no tables; suitable central décor; candle lighting. Tea/coffee was available as people arrived; each was welcomed; name badges were distributed. All these things helped to form community. Humour also helped!

At 10.10 a.m. there was a formal welcome by the PP, who sketched the project and the progress of discussions to date. It was understood that all had read up on the material he had distributed. No clarifications were in fact requested. He stressed that this meeting would be deliberative: that he would accept whatever outcome emerged as final. (5 mins)

I then welcomed the group, saying:

You may well be asking 'Why am I here?' It can be a shock to know that this decision lies with you. What you decide is the way things will be. This level of responsibility is new in the Church. But we are here as a community of faith: the three divine Persons are with us and will help us if we are open to them. Bidden or unbidden, God is present (Jung). We will pray our way together to a decision: God will lead us to what is best, if we are open. We are here on behalf of this parish and of the wider People of God.

Now a word on communal discernment. Pope Francis in The Joy of the Gospel speaks of Communal Discernment as the way forward for the Church; this is the way it will face its challenges on all levels. So we are making ecclesiastical history! But of course this way of arriving at good decisions has a long history and has taken many forms. Think of the last Conclave that elected Pope Francis: how did it run? The participants shared on the current needs of the Church; they prayed and discussed; they voted as they felt God was prompting them and finally reached the required majority. Then all showed their acceptance of the choice and promised their support to the new Pope. They ended with a prayer of Thanksgiving. We will be doing something like that. Any comments? (10 mins)

So let us pray and put God at the centre of our meeting.

O God, from whom all good things come, grant that we, who call on you in our need, may at your prompting discern what is right, and by your guidance do it. We ask this though Christ our Lord, Amen.

FORMAT

'We'll use the following format: Firstly I will speak briefly about myself and my role; then I will help you to become a team that can work together easily. Next we will clarify issues around the project.

We will then look at our Vision for the parish, and ask 'Does the project enhance/forward our agreed vision?' We will do this, not by debate but by gathering all the arguments FOR the project; then the arguments AGAINST it. We will then take a break! When we return I will lead a short time of prayer during which I will invite you to ask God to direct your heart to what is best.

Then comes the vote: it will be secret, so you can feel free to vote as your conscience suggests. I will not be voting, because I am neutral. I hope the vote will bring us to a consensus: if not, we will need to go back a bit and listen further to one another! We will wrap up the morning by thanking God for bringing us to our decision; then we will discuss the steps needed to implement it. Finally I will ask you to notice what you have learnt from the exercise. We will, I hope, end before 13.00, in time for a good lunch and even a glass of wine!' (5 mins)

I then said what was needed about myself and about my role as facilitator. (2 mins)

COMMUNITY

'We need to become a working community for the duration of this discernment. I want everyone to feel at ease and to trust that their contributions will be respected. We need to be FOR each other, so we need to know where others are coming from and in what ways they are invested in this issue. Here are a few training exercises!

> ➤ I ask you first to stand and move toward someone you don't know well and share on the question: 'How did you get involved in the parish or the project?' (5 mins)
> ➤ I invite you now to sit and to notice if you have any image of the group. Are we like pilgrims at a crossroad? Or a football team, ready to go? Or a herd of sheep? Or like the Hebrews in the desert? (The group shared its images, a few of which were hilarious). (8 mins)

- ➢ Now go to someone else whom you don't know well and share on the question: 'What do I bring to the group?' (8 mins)
- ➢ Now a silent pause: no sharing! Ask yourself, 'Have I any prejudices which could spoil the good working of the group?' Is there anyone here I don't like or trust? Do I feel close to God or distant?' (5 mins)
- ➢ Finally take a moment to pray that you may not get in the way of the Good Spirit. The Spirit is in the group looking around for someone who is paying attention to his gestures. Can you wave your hand at him? Try doing that now! (2 mins)

THE PROJECT

The persons behind the project spoke briefly. Clarifications were given until all agreed that they had the needed facts, including the financial implications. (10 mins)

THE PARISH VISION

The Parish Vision Statement was read, plus a section from *The Joy of the Gospel* on the parish as a centre of Evangelisation. People buzzed on this, then shared in the group. Next they were asked to consider quietly whether the project would enhance the Vision (10 mins)

FOR/AGAINST

Each participant wrote down on their jotter all the points they could think of in favour of the project. These were shared and written up by the secretary on a flip chart. Likewise the points against it (10 mins)

BREAK AT 11.30.

'No lobbying during this time! Chat as you wish but keep an open mind until the moment of voting. Be like a balance at equilibrium!' (20 mins)

PRAYER

'Thanks for coming back! We have done what we could to grasp the pro's and con's for the project. Now God must draw our hearts to what is best, so let us pray. St Ignatius has a homely image of a cook that I find helpful around this time of prayer! The cook wonders what the master wants for dinner: no amount of discussion with the kitchen staff will tell him. He must ask the man himself. So he goes into the master's study with beef on one plate and fish on the other. The master says nothing, but the cook keeps his eyes on his face until he sees which dish gets the nod. I invite you to imagine God present to you; ask God to move your heart in the way he wants. You could pray, 'Speak, Lord; your servant is listening. Not my will but yours be done!' Then try to notice what way your heart is being drawn. You may feel that saying Yes to the proposed project brings you energy and peace, and that saying No leaves you flat and discontented. Or perhaps the opposite.' (10 mins).

VOTE

Voting procedures were clarified.

'A simple majority is sought. If there is a tied vote, we will adjourn and then ask people what is going on for them, then move along again. If we do have a consensus we will spend some little time at least to see if any concern of the minority can be included in the final decision. This will help to gain greater support for the decision. Cards will now be distributed: just write Yes or No. The secretary will collect the cards and count them. I then announce the result.' (8 mins)

The vote was eighteen in favour and two against. Those who had voted against said that they were willing to go with the majority once they had been reassured on certain points.

IMPLEMENTATION STRATEGIES
Agreement was reached on who does what and when. (5 mins)

THANKSGIVING
I led a short prayer of thanks (1) to God for leading us; (2) for one another and the generous engagement with the process; (3) and for bringing us to consensus and then to unanimity (2 mins)

HARVESTING OUR LEARNINGS
> 'What have we learnt about communal discernment? Does it build community? Is there any better way than this for the Church to move forward?
> Has God become closer and more real? God has been journeying with us, and leading us towards life. Do we sense that we have been collaborating with God? Are we grateful?
> What have I learnt about myself? God chose me for this present task and met me personally today! God met the others too, which brings me to a new respect and reverence for them. What gifts and skills did I bring to the discernment?
> We made a corporate decision, so we are all in this project together! We will follow through by promoting it to others. We won't despair in difficulties or become negative' (15 mins).

CLOSURE
The Parish Priest closed the meeting at 12.45 p.m. Lunch followed. There was a strong sense of community: as one man put it, *We've been through something big together!*

 God journeys with us and leads us towards life.

III. POPE FRANCIS' SYNODS

The jury is out on whether the Synod on the Family in October 2015 was a success or failure. According to one commentator, 'Since it was instituted by Pope Paul VI the synod has never been a "dynamic" body, according to Pope Francis himself, and this one was no different. Nothing new or interesting has emerged'. Pope Francis himself in his concluding address to the synod members expressed a level of frustration in referring to 'closed hearts' which hide behind the Church's teachings, sit on the chair of Moses and pass judgement on others, sometimes with superiority and superficiality. In his closing homily he criticised the attitude which does not want to be bothered by the problems of others: 'In this way we are with Jesus but we do not think like him … Our hearts are not open … We live far from his heart … We already have our schedule … Every problem is a bother.'

The synod's outcomes will disappoint some and encourage others. But it is worth looking behind the scenes to see what was really going on: my contention is that no matter what the specific outcomes, the very event of the Synod with its open atmosphere was a massive achievement.

VATICAN II

The participants at Vatican II, 1962-1965, opened up the Catholic Church to the reality of change and development, but they saw that structures were needed to enable the process of *aggiornamento* to continue. Without these they knew that the Church would continue its habit of arriving – if at all – breathless and a little late, and that it would react defensively rather than gracefully to the signs of the times. So the bishops proposed the establishment of a synod with a rotating membership which would work steadily with the pope to secure authentic development within the Church. 'Synod' means 'to walk together' so it was to be expected that the 'pilgrim Church' would wend its way at a pace suited to the majority rather than to those out in front or lagging behind. Over the years since Vatican II a number of synods were held, but their role was advisory; debate was limited, and the final documents written by successive popes were criticised as doing less than full justice to the expressed views of the participants.

A NEW STYLE

The style of Pope Francis' synods has shown a radical step forward from what has gone before, and that is their great achievement. Francis is a Jesuit, and the Jesuits were founded through a communal discernment, of which the details are fully available. It is not surprising therefore that the key dynamic of his synods is likewise *communal discernment*. In his November 2013 Apostolic Exhortation, *The Joy of the Gospel*, the pope uses the term itself more than twenty times. It is, he says, the way forward on all levels in the Church:

> *Discernment will entail allowing ourselves to be guided by the Holy Spirit, renouncing the attempt to plan and control everything to the last detail, and instead letting the Spirit enlighten, guide and direct us* (288).

'What's new?' one may ask: 'surely that is how the Church is always meant to act?' Yes, indeed, but often the required dispositions are lacking in the participants.

HUMBLE SEARCHING

What is communal discernment at its best? It occurs when a group tries to search together for what God may want. To search is not yet to possess what is being sought, and to maintain a closed mind and heart in the search is to impede the work of the Spirit. Communal discernment leaves no place for pride or dogmatism, for aggressiveness or defensiveness, for lobbying or bullying. Instead, discussion and debate have a tentative quality: *'I wonder ...' 'It seems to me ...' 'Explain your idea a bit more to me ...'*

Good listening becomes more important than good talking. Each participant tries to put a good interpretation on what others offer, rather than rubbishing it. In this way negativity and hostility diminish. Everyone feels that they are being heard, even if not agreed with. The blind spots, biases and prejudices of others become obvious: but instead of despairing of the process, *personal* examination of conscience becomes important. Each can ask, *'Where am I closing myself to the truth?'* The more sincerely everyone engages with the process, the more does inner freedom emerge. Instead of remaining defensive of their sincerely held views, all move towards wanting what God wants.

A GROUP THAT IS LED

Instead of arguing over opposing views, the participants begin to see themselves as a group of disciples who want to be enlightened by the Holy Spirit. It is not lobbying or the loudest voice that carries the day, but the quiet voice that somehow carries the echo of the Spirit's prompting and offers a revelatory moment in which the right way forward is seen. Instead of endless talking, participants give time to prayer and ask for openness to the truth. They ask themselves the radical question: 'Which of the available options seems best to express Gospel values?'

Instead of a Government/Opposition approach, all the members explore together the arguments in favour of the option under consideration, then the arguments against it. This strategy transcends opposing views and softens the debate. In this phase creativity and leadership are needed: the group needs persons with imagination who can craft amendments that carry the best of the contributions that have been made. When there is no more to be said, members take time out to pray for light to see which side of the option brings energy and a sense of congruence, and which side seems to drain energy away and cause fragmentation.

At the close, ideally there are no winners or losers, no animosities, no dissatisfied minorities. Communal discernment includes but goes beyond democracy. Instead, woven out of divine and human effort, there emerges a consensus that this or that option seems best to serve the good of those who will be affected by the decision to be made. When the contentious issue of criteria for admission of pagans to the Christian community was resolved, those signing off on it could write, '*It has seemed good to the Holy Spirit and to us ...*' (Acts 15:28).

COMMUNITY

Communal discernment is a cleansing task: its reward is a disposition of openness to the truth which blows where it will. When the manifold elements in communal discernment are allowed to operate, genuine community is established: respect and love grow as the search continues, and this bonding often turns out to be of more lasting value than the particular decisions that are agreed. Groups that engage once in communal discernment will want to return to the process again and again, as their best way to move forward in challenging situations.

RESPECT FOR THE TRUTH

Was the synod of 2015 a success or failure? The initial dispositions of the participants constituted a spectrum from the hard left to the hard right. From the reports, it appears that many warmed to the discipline of communal discernment at least in some of its elements. Everyone had the opportunity to speak freely, and the sincere and principled clash of views must have broadened the minds of those prepared to listen. One hopes that everyone felt not only heard but respected. In the decisions made, enough wiggle room is present so that contentious issues can be pursued further.

The Church is led slowly into the truth: it would be naïve to expect that all the neuralgic issues besetting the Church could be sorted out in a single synod. What matters is that a significant step forward has been taken and that a process that began in the early Church with the first Council of Jerusalem in 50 AD has been restored to centre stage. The synod's style has something to say to the wider world too: the dynamics of communal discernment can be helpful to decision makers of any persuasion. What matters is that those involved should be willing to walk together in searching for the best way forward in challenging situations. As a patristic adage has it: '*In necessary matters there must be unity; in doubtful matters, liberty; in all things, love.*'

# SUGGESTIONS FOR FURTHER READING

Wilkie Au and Noreen Au, *The Discerning Heart: Exploring the Christian Path*, NY: Paulist, 2006.

Dean Brackley SJ, *The Call to Discernment in Troubled Times*, New York: Crossroad, 2004.

Pope Francis, *The Joy of the Gospel*, Dublin: Veritas, 2013.

Pope Francis: *Laudato Si': On Care for Our Common Home*, Dublin: Veritas, 2015.

Elizabeth Liebert, *The Way of Discernment: Spiritual Practices for Decision-Making*, London: John Knox Press, 2008.

J. A. Munitiz SJ and P. Endean SJ, *St Ignatius of Loyola: Personal Writings*, London: Penguin, 2004.

J. M. Sparough, J. Manney and T. Hipskind SJ, *What's Your Decision?* Chicago: Loyola Press, 2010.

Teilhard de Chardin SJ, *The Divine Milieu*, London: Collins, 1960.

G. W. Traub SJ, *An Ignatian Spirituality Reader*, Chicago: Loyola Press, 2008.

Joseph Veale SJ, *Manifold Gifts*, Oxford: Way Books, 2006.

Pope Francis Biographies

> Leonardo Boff, *Francis of Rome and Francis of Assisi*, New York: Orbis, 2014.
> Paul Vallely, *Pope Francis, Untying the Knots*, (Second edition) London: Bloomsbury, 2015.
> Austen Ivereigh, *The Great Reformer: Francis and the Making of a Radical Pope*, London: Allen & Unwin, 2014.

Many websites are available on Ignatian spirituality. Start perhaps with www.jesuit.ie or www.ignatianspirituality.com.

In this book, I have touched lightly on themes that are more developed in my other books: *Reflective Living; Love Beyond All Telling; Our Graced Life-Stories; Finding God in All Things* (all Messenger Publications); *Meetings Matter; Alone and on Foot; Where to from Here?* (all Veritas Publications).